Budtender Education:
Cannabis Education for Budtenders
an Oakland Equity Perspective.
Series I
Volume 1

By Javier Armas

Budtender Education:

Cannabis Education for Budtenders an Oakland

Equity Perspective

by Javier Armas

Oakland, CA

December 4th, 2020

Illustrator Art by DJ Sosa

Budtender Education: Volume 1, Series 1.

Published by Javier's Organics,

an Official Oakland Equity Cannabis Business

ISBN: 978-1-7362782-1-5

<u>Budtender Education:</u>

Cannabis Education for Budtenders from an Oakland Equity Perspective by Javier Armas

Oakland, CA

December 4th, 2020

Table of Contents

INTRODUCTION

"I need something to help me sleep" is a common request patients have for Budtenders, those serving cannabis products behind the counter at cannabis dispensaries. Budtenders are the key industrial human link between Brands and patients within cannabis retail. As more states legalize cannabis, more dispensaries form, hiring those to sell cannabis to patients. More and more people find themselves in a new profession, as a Budtender. Who educates and trains the Budtenders to help patients? Do medical officials educate Budtenders about insomnia, cancer, or other illnesses? Do dispensaries have professional relationships with hospitals? Unfortunately, no because of the federal criminalization of cannabis. There is a lack of educational training in cannabis. Federal criminalization of cannabis created the lack of a standard scientific and historical knowledge of cannabis. With a rapid legalization movement state by state, thousands of people are becoming Budtenders overnight, without the necessary training and education. As a result, tension arises at the point of exchange with patient medical needs not being met by the young industry. I dedicate this Budtender Education book series to addressing and challenging that problem, offering cutting edge quality educational cannabis content.

I created this book by work experience with over one hundred cannabis retailers in California, with strong relationships with managers and budtenders, the glue of the industry, with extensive research over all the key issues cannabis is facing. We will start with why Budtender Education is an important movement, and the original conditions that birthed its concept. With accessing quality cannabis education, we will start with the Canadian University Lethbridge's study on cannabis and COVID. Budtenders should be familiar with this study, concluding the number #1 effective strain contained a 27 to 1 CBD to THC ratio in slowing down COVID-19. The most important article in this book is Unearthing a New Cannabis Business Model, the beginning vision of a new system, the inspiration for the rest of the writings that proceeded, the spinal cord role for the book. This is followed up by engaging in business cannabis analysis, why are some of the big names in cannabis failing, and how does that shift our perspective on cannabis business development?

Politics is no doubt built into cannabis due to the criminalization of the plant. With approximately 40,000 people in prison for cannabis, many being Black, Latino, and working class, still in jail, the engine of profiting from cannabis can't ignore this history when shaping contemporary cannabis policies. References to Equity Cannabis businesses are companies that cities officially recognize as meeting a criteria that demonstrates being negatively impacted by the war on drugs, which were deeply racial in character. Equity cannabis companies have been negatively impacted by the war on drugs. Oakland, San Francisco, Sacramento, Los Angeles, and Long Beach are cities that have instituted or partly instituted this program, with more counties like Humbodt and Mendocino planning to follow suit. This book represents the beginning of a new genre of writing, from an equity cannabis perspective, engaging the emerging and forming regulatory cannabis legal system through the lens of the harsh past damages that ravaged inner cities throughout the US.

Cannabis has other important political facets; the compassionate program with legislation SB 34, free cannabis programs for those that need it, cannabis, and the essential farm workers during COVID. Also, $30 million in California state equity funds for equity cannabis businesses, Lebanon's struggle to legalize cannabis, how we use cannabis to justify police brutality, the role of the late justice Ruth Bader Ginsburg within changing cannabis law, and indigenous knowledge of wildfires for farming stability. Offering a multi-dimensional unique analysis, we will look at how nature and society interplay, offering ecologically inspired analysis to business and political problems. With the criminalization of cannabis, it is political, and it is important we offer a perspective that helps Budtenders handle all the exploding issues at hand and its moving political parts.

As an Oakland native and Bay Area Cannabis operator, I wanted to offer a nuanced cutting edge analysis of local policy. Recognizing the openings for change, city council members are the most open to proposed cannabis policies from its constituents. Mobilizing on the local level can be effective, encouraging the cannabis community to increase its political organizing work and utilize these openings to build more sensible cannabis policies. If Budtenders build communities that engage in local political activism across California, it could tilt the balance of forces, helping complete sensible policy we need to accomplish, such as lowering the high taxes and amending the hyper regulations. Budtenders could also open spaces to express what they are passionate about changing regarding the industry, armed with a nuanced perspective. With that said, there are six articles on Bay Area cannabis policies capturing important events officials of Santa Clara County, the Cities of San Jose, Berkeley, and Oakland had with cannabis businesses.

Three articles on California Cannabis law are to help understand the California cannabis legal system, focused on organic agriculture, and geographically labeled appellations. These articles are to add foundational understanding of the supply chain most budtenders are not exposed to, agriculture. The ending is on cannabis and grief; as we know, we often use alcohol in times of sorrow, and we should explore how cannabis can play an effective role during challenging times.

I was a Budtender from 2004-07, and now I am an official Oakland equity Cannabis business owner of Javier's Organics. Oakland is a leader in reversing the damages of the war on drugs created, demonstrating local political leadership for cannabis that other city governments around the world could look to. This book is to partly inspire a local cannabis democratic movement for change across the globe by peeking into and learning from the California Cannabis industry with an Oakland equity perspective. I do this as my small part in building equity and equality within cannabis, uniquely combining the strength of Oakland's achievements and the agency of education. The education offered to Budtenders creates a movement of empowerment, reflecting the values built into the cannabis plant itself.

Javier Armas,
Oakland, CA

THE MISSION

1. Budtender Education as a Movement

Photo Credit: JASON SWEENEY | Bay Area News Group, East Bay Times

PUBLISHED: October 31, 2007

"Let me see all your top purple 1/8ths," a patient would ask, behind a bulletproof window, a metallic hole for communication, with fifteen people in line looking over. "We have Purple Haze, Purple Crush, Purple Factory, and Grand Daddy." "Which is the one?" the patient would ask. "The Purple Factory is exceptional in smell and taste, and the Grand Daddy is hitting super hard," I would respond, as the patient intensely looked close into the four different bags, isolating the two to choose from. "I will take this one," the patient responded, and I would collect the money. I did this work during and right after college. The cultures of the budtenders were street smart, encyclopedic knowledge of cannabis strains, decked out in Bay Area sports gear. Many of them had their own Hip Hop CDs independently published. The Compassionate Collective of Alameda County "CCAC," in Hayward,

11

operated from 2003-2007, serving hundreds of thousands of Bay Area patients, shutdown by the DEA.[1] We all dealt with an array of street characters and seriously ill patients with never a dull moment, and the exchange was not always simple. There was a skill set where embodying product knowledge and customer service work melted into a common rhythm.

Shortly after, I became a History High School teacher for the Oakland Unified School District. My teaching credential required studying the method of teaching, also called Pedagogy. Due to the criminalization of cannabis in education, there was zero pedagogy with cannabis based curriculum. The underdeveloped cannabis retail world meeting standardized education inspired me to build Budtender Education.

I spent five years teaching History in Oakland, connecting to thousands of incredible young people, with many now being in the cannabis industry. Teaching is a difficult task that requires dedication, repetition, and commitment, as well as analyzing the complexity of each individual. I studied Malcolm X's chapter Saved in his autobiography, how he learned to read, and how he ended up reading the whole library in prison. I also studied Russian Psychologist Lev Vygotsky, whose theory on cognitive development was social interaction is fundamental for growth, and it creates what he calls "a zone of proximal development." Utilizing these influences, I tried to create a new learning framework for Oakland youth. As time went on, I switched careers and entered law.

I became a Civil Rights paralegal and then jumped in wage and hour law. I saw how immigrants were getting ripped off at work and learned how to apply California employment legal provisions for workers' rights, filing for over a million dollars in damages from lack of legal pay with the California Department of Labor Standards Enforcement "DLSE." I learned

1 Federal agents raid marijuana dispensary by JASON SWEENEY | Bay Area News Group, East Bay Times October 31, 2007

civil rights laws working on police brutality cases; looking at the pictures from police reports from some of the police brutality cases were horrifying. Employment and Civil Rights law put together could be powerful and are not as combined as I thought they would be. As proposition 64 passed, I saw to distribute the professional civil rights law knowledge into the emerging cannabis industry to create a more equitable business environment.

I jumped into cannabis sales and excelled, utilizing my paralegal skills for sharp documentation to help the process of completing orders. But on the retail end, if the Budtenders did not know what the product was for and what value it brought, the sales would be slow and burdensome for storage. As a response, I jumped into retail product education, executing them at stores in San Francisco, Richmond, Berkeley, Oakland, San Jose, and Santa Cruz, doing 15-20 minute presentations with groups of 5-10 Budtenders. At the end of my product based presentation, I had a surprise. I pulled out several history books on cannabis. I summarized each one in 30 seconds, giving them an introductory presentation to cannabis history. In 2020, I pivoted to a digital-focused on the spot journalist cannabis writing due to COVID. This book is the natural maturation of such educational retail work.

Integrating ecological, legal, and political analysis into articles that regularly get circulated in the cannabis industry, hundreds of Budtenders have read such articles and shown their appreciation. Budtender Neeno Laflex, awarded the 2019 Budtender of the Year Award, stated, " these articles are amazing educational tools for anyone in the cannabis industry, especially budtenders." The support and encouragement from Bay Area Budtenders, like Neeno Laflex, from 2017 to the present, and the agreement of the need for quality accessible cannabis education has created a movement. Budtender Education's writings is a crystalized expression of such a young movement. The movement of empowerment by reclaiming independent thought with healthy intellectual practices. Corporations can attempt to capture market share within the Cannabis Educational Industry, but if the authors never worked in cannabis, the content will be flat, lacking life. A Veteran Budtender's production of quality educational Cannabis content is dynamic and organic with a higher alignment with the energetic frequency of the plant and a deeper appreciation and connection for the farmer. Budtenders producing original writing is part of this movement; those that consume, work in cannabis retail, and engage hundreds of patients a day have powerful insights for the industry to grow with health and success.

SCIENCE

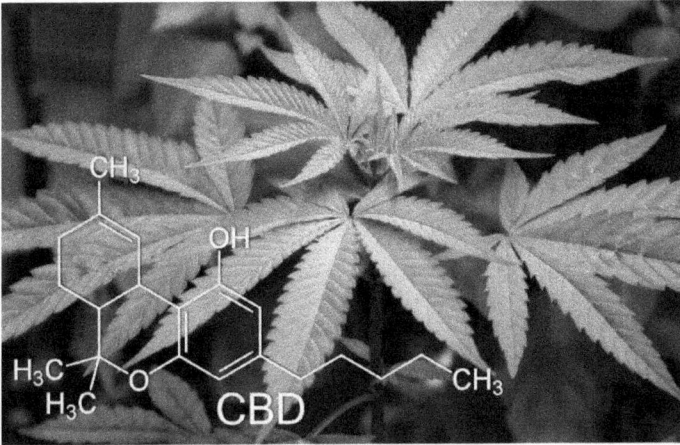

2.Scientists show Cannabis can slow down the Coronavirus.

"Working under the Health Canada research license, we have developed over 800 new Cannabis sativa lines and extracts and hypothesized that high-CBD C. sativa extracts may be used to modulate ACE2 expression in COVID19 target tissues."

In Search of Preventative Strategies: Novel Anti-inflammatory High-CBD Cannabis Sativa Extracts Modulate ACE2 Expression in COVID-19 Gateway Tissues

by University of Lethbridge

Cannabis science grew in force when Canadian University Lethbridge published a study showing how cannabis strains with high CBD can slow down the coronavirus. The scientists studied over 400 strains, focusing on a select dozen with high levels of CBD. The study directly stated, "If further confirmed, select high-CBD cannabis extracts can be used to develop prevention strategies directed at lowering or modulating ACE2 levels in high-risk tissues." By using oral, airway, and intestinal tissues, using artificial human 3-D tissue models, they analyzed how each strain impacted COVID-19 infections. This is exciting and cutting edge medical data that will mature the cannabis industry worldwide.

The lead researcher, biological scientist Dr. Igor Kovalchuk, stated[2] some strains showed promising results as they reduced the virus receptors by 73%. According to Kovalchuk, "Several them have reduced the number of these (virus) receptors by 73 %, the chance of it getting in is much lower. If they can reduce the number of receptors, there's much less chance of getting infected." This does not mean cannabis will create a vaccine, but it will be a contribution to preventative medicine. The conclusion of the study states:

Based on our preliminary data, extracts of novel efficacious C. sativa lines, pending further investigations, may become a useful addition to the treatment of COVID-19 and an excellent GRAS adjunct therapy. They may also be used to develop additional easy-to-use preventative strategies such as mouth wash and throat gargle products that may be tested for their potential to decrease viral entry via the oral cavity and may be used both in clinical practice and at-home treatment.[3]

---

2 Cannabis shows promise blocking coronavirus infection: Alberta researcher by Bill Kaufmann May 07, 2020
3 In Search of Preventative Strategies: Novel Anti Inflammatory High-CBD Cannabis Sativa Extracts Modulate ACE2 Expression in COVID-19 Gateway Tissues Bo Wang, Anna Kovalchuk, Dongping Li1, Yaroslav Ilnytskyy, Igor Kovalchuk and Olga Kovalchuk. Page 5 for Table 1.

Scientists show Cannabis can slow down the Coronavirus.

Table 1. Content of major cannabinoids – THC and CBD, and THC: CBD ratios in tested C. sativa lines.

Extract	THC	CBD	THC:CBD ratio
#1	0.25%	6.79%	1:27
#5	0.25%	8.5%	1:35
#7	0.21%	7.2%	1:34
#9	0.22%	6.91%	1:31
#10	0.45%	9.5%	1:21
#31	4.5%	6.7%	1:1.5
#45	0.03%	1.61%	1:54
#49	0.15%	3.1%	1:9
#81	0.55%	11.5%	1:21
#90	0.99%	4.58%	1:5
#114	0.22%	6.8%	1:31
#115	0.4%	9.54%	1:24
#129	0.34%	6.75%	1:20
#130	0.86%	2.63%	1:3
#131	0.44%	6.1%	1:14
#155	0.22%	4.59%	1:21
#157	0.2%	3.78%	1:19
#166	0.1%	2.5%	1:25
#167	0.08%	2.25%	1:28
#169	0.21%	1.88%	1:9
#207	4.34%	4.68%	1:1
#274	0.44%	9.02%	1:21

Lines indicated in bold have less then 0.3% of total THC and therefore can be classified as CBD Hemp in Canada and USA. Lines that were shown to affect ACE2 expression (Fig. 2-4) are indicated in red.

We can see the most medically effective ratios have high CBD concentration. The number #1 effective ratio was 1 part THC to 27 part CBD, closely followed up by a 1 to 35, 1 to 34, and 1 to 31 THC to CBD extract ratios. High CBD with low THC ratios demonstrated medicinal impact, but the study has not yet captured medicinal data of the other cannabinoids besides THC and CBD. Cannabis has 100 phytocannabinoids 22 of delta-9- tetrahydrocannabinol (Δ-THC), what gets you high, and 23 are cannabidiol (CBD) that is medicinal, which means there are over 55 more cannabinoids with other unknown medicinal Cannabinoids yet to be discovered by science. Each cannabinoid has its own effect, THC gets you high, CBD is medicinal and anti-inflammatory, CBN makes you sleepy, but when the cannabinoids work together as a whole, it embodies a full-spectrum dynamic. Many full spectrum cannabis products with medicinal value, such as Rick Simpson Oil "RSO," are engineered to be full spectrum.

Many old landraces are high in CBD, lower in THC, like what is in the Bekaa Valley of Lebanon, Panama Red, or Afghani. Preserving ancient strains for their medicinal properties is key work needed by those dedicated to the preservation of the spirit of cannabis. We never know when a rare ancient strain might have the perfect formulation of cannabinoids and terpenes for a specific human ailment. On top of ancient strains and the cannabinoids in the plant, we have different terpene profiles, which also have their own unique medicinal qualities, odors, and tastes. The foundation is the biodiversity of the soil that generates such terpenes and cannabinoids. From cannabinoids, terpenes, and the soil's biodiversity, the composition of cannabis is rich and complex, with enormous amounts of medicinal properties to be discovered by science. Many cannabis veterans intuitively know this, which drives their hard work and self-dedication towards the young industry.

As craft farmers struggle against the large, capitalized farms, small cannabis businesses compete with large corporations, cannabis oriented scientists have marginalized in a pharmaceutical shaped political environment where cannabis science is taboo. Cutting edge science unearthing the medicinal power of cannabis is a politically powerful shift that can alter legal barriers and negative cultural assumptions. For us, the question is, how can we build closer ties to such leading scientists to form a collaborative environment where we train Budtenders to have a standard medical cannabis science.

Scientists show Cannabis can slow down the Coronavirus.

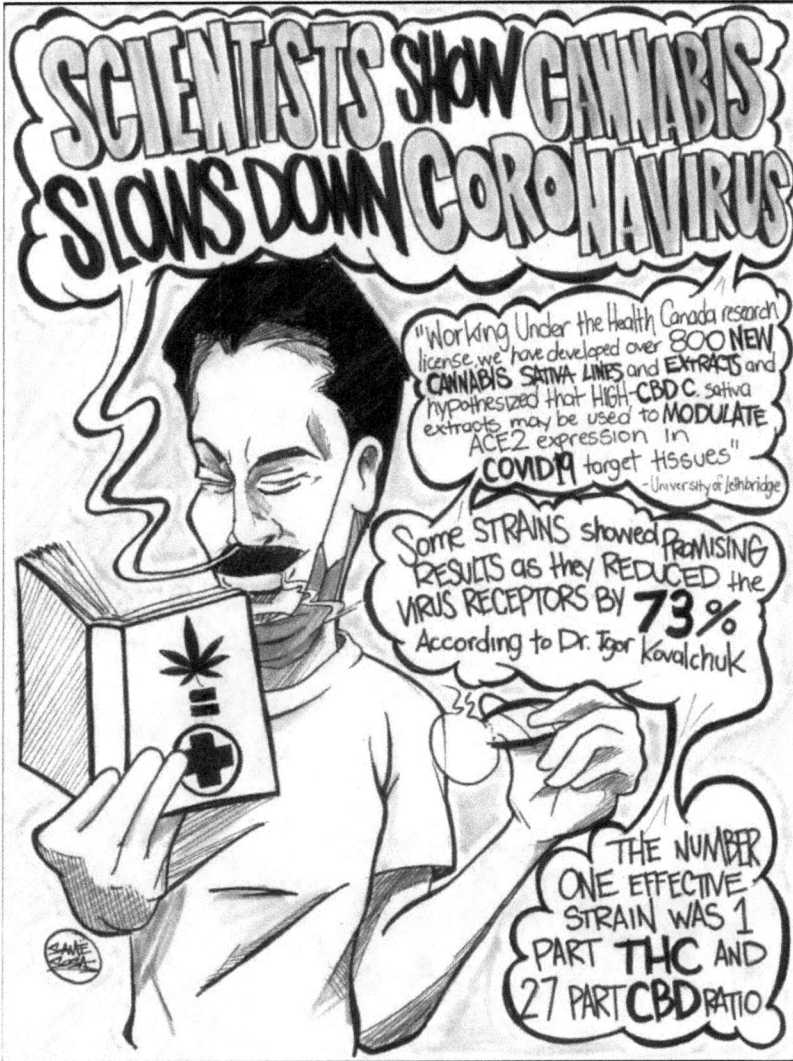

BUSINESS ANALYSIS

3.Unearthing a New Cannabis Business Model for California

As an Oakland equity cannabis business grounded in cannabis retail, I want to offer a unique perspective on the difficulties the cannabis industry is facing. Countless articles have pointed to the high taxes and a strong illicit market, as well as many cities and counties not allowing for cannabis businesses to form as central barriers to market growth, which of course, they are. I want to dig a little deeper than the obvious issues at hand. The 2018 recreational market rush has slowed down, and multiple corporations have downsized. Small companies have gone out of business, all of which demands that we need a more mature intervention for long-term business success.

Many non-cannabis industry professionals thought their mechanical application of business knowledge would outperform the alleged "stoner" business world of prop 215. Heavily capitalized companies boldly advertised in their pursuit for market share. Such practices included the billboard frenzy, skyrocketing the advertisement cost of sales to enormous levels, making margins impossible in the immediate. But the idea is to capture market share now, and let margins develop later. Brands on the market are constantly getting challenged. Established buyers for brick and mortars cannabis dispensaries report they receive an email a minute from vendors. The buyers know most patients or customers have little to no brand loyalty, and they need to compete with their neighboring brick and mortar cannabis dispensaries, who also are pitched by the same brands. In working class communities, price point drives sales. I will ask the buyer, "what do you sell the most of?" "$20 1/8s out the door," is the response, which means they are buying them for approximately $8 a 1/8th from a wholesaler. Brands have yet to carry weight in many of these places. Undercutting via price is the name of the game for much of the market dynamics, even with top shelf products. A few brands are rising slightly above this dynamic but still struggle with the competition to make their margins. Most capitalized companies will offer promotions, buy one get one for a dollar, but this is a temporary tactic to capture market share and pull out once the brand is rooted. The problem is another company is ready to replace such a "rooted" company with parallel quality, price, and aggressive promotions. So many of the biggest names in cannabis are not making any profit, operating in the red, while for the customer, it creates a hurricane-like dynamic, appearing to be chaos in the market.[4]

As big as the California cannabis market is, it's small. It's one of the first things a retail buyer will tell you. The struggle for brand recognition is real, and not one company has mastered a formula for it. January 2018 to the present has been a field of experiments, rich with lessons. Fundamentally, reputation is key, especially considering the world of buyers is relatively small. Buyers need a good reason to bring a new product or SKU to market, and most complain about "new" products being merely rebranded old ones with only a better price point or different packaging and marketing. Capitalized companies also exert aggression towards market share, creating pressures on the buyers that bleeds into the relations with the whole brick and mortar staff. Any laxed attitude in sales gets you cut out of the game. It's a fine balance. Most budtenders making $15 - $20 an hour have a high level influence over store purchases. They display a natural sympathy with the small craft company on a political level but in daily practice, they often push deals and promotions from heavily capitalized companies because it's the best deal of the day for the customer. We can see branding recognition finds itself in a difficult position, caught between craft integrity and value centered purchases. We also see an opening where if craft companies can play ball like the heavily capitalized ones, even on a local level, it could capture the best of both worlds. But with slim margins and heavy operating costs, every move needs to be seriously calculated.

---

4 See more vividly on how companies are struggling with margins; What cannabis industry CEOs need to survive 2020 Published January 17, 2020 | By Codie Sanchez

The heavily capitalized companies overspent building their foundation, only to execute mass layoffs in the recent period.

Building a foundation is key. If buyers can see integrity in your work, and your product, it doesn't matter if you have a staff of only three people with only 100 marketing flyers. This is how investment can't build on itself and will only burn if it tries. As someone that takes the essence of cannabis seriously, I think about what we can learn from ecological structures of growth and reproduction, and how that can help us form a different business model that doesn't waste resources, is not scared of slow growth, and knows how to work with the nuances of each microclimate retail environment. The knowledge of seasoned budtenders knows how product moves and what product moves, key nuances. Detailed data is often blurred from meta-strategies but understood intuitively by hard-working sales representatives. With too many meta shots in the game that lack precision, every company needs to have a clear answer to what value they offer the industry and know a low price point only holds temporary water. Such value can have many forms and creative cutting edge entrepreneurs who will capture this unique opening.

4. The California Cannabis Industry Struggles for a Vision

Companies like MedMen and INSA may have decided that they've already cracked the code, but it remains to be seen whether that's even possible with a plant as complex as cannabis.

Gary Greenberg, New York Times. April 13, 2020

The California Cannabis industry faces historically unparalleled challenges. Building successful business models are as bleak. First high taxes, massive destructive fires, then strict METRC regulations, massive layoffs, corporations failing, with a Coronavirus pandemic to top it off. As mentioned, no brand has cracked the code with a successful business model. The quickly changing products, creating menu complexity with a hyper-competitive environment. It creates quick-shifting sands that devour classic business foundations. As human health via our respiratory systems are under pandemic attack, a clear short term and long term market approach are needed.

Reports have shown extracts have declined in sales, the flow is steady, and edibles have had a huge upsurge. Smoking, dabbing, eating, and drinking has had different health impacts under the pandemic. The health of one's home under quarantine is the epicenter, and consuming cannabis in a respiratory, healthy way has become central to our new reality. Brick and Mortar Cannabis dispensaries are also not the hot business place it once was, with vaping lounges closed and deliveries ramping up in market share.

Unfortunately, brands and the medical cannabis community are too far apart for this to happen quickly.

The American Journal of Endocannabinoid Medicine, which helps educate medical professionals on the role of the endocannabinoid system and medical cannabis, is launching its first certification for healthcare professionals. An outstanding fact as of 2020, only 9% of medical schools offer medical cannabis in their curriculum. If they suppressed Cannabis science in medical school, then it is suppressed in society at large. Programs that offer this type of training, independent of brands and grounded in science, will help the industry mature in leaps and bounds. "This professional certification in endocannabinoid medicine is very different from training offerings in the hemp-CBD, medical cannabis, and cannabinoid pharma market, in that it was developed with the independence and integrity required for ACCME-accredited education of physicians"[5], said Jahan Marcu, Ph.D., editor-in-chief of the American Journal of Endocannabinoid Medicine.

Raising the medical standards of cannabis knowledge and practice is key as thousands of patients have picked their cannabis product without any medical insight as well as the thousands of budtenders who make choices based on samples and brand-based "education" with information generated from brands marketing teams. California shapes their cannabis menus by the metrics of commercial products and processed foods.. A deeper scientific knowledge of how to unleash the medical potential of cannabis will reshape and create new products. Applying strains with certain terpene balances will mix favorably with certain herbal and root foods, ginger, mango, cinnamon. The medical value of such products will be much higher with comparable costs in production. History has a rich record, the ancient Indian's created Bhang around 2,000 BC, where cannabis was mixed with several plant-

---

5 Endocannabinoid Medicine Certification Syllabus of April 2020

based foods to use as a sacred drink for special ceremonies. Their cannabis landraces had a higher CBD and a lower THC, creating a full-spectrum medical impact. Utilizing past historical developments, the rich biodiversity of California soil and contemporary medical cannabis science are the ingredients for the breakthroughs the industry longs for.

Cracking the code is possible, but not without industrial resilience, with a complex analysis that incorporates agriculture, endocannabinoid science, human anatomy, high taxes, a fragmented cannabis culture, all within a pandemic shaped environment. As the accumulation of extreme pressure forms crystals, industry leaders will arise, producing a vision that is directly out of that terrain of tension.

5. Failing Giants and Natural Alternatives: Cannabis Seeks a new Business Model

How can the cannabis industry succeed? If we analyze the business model of some of the giants of cannabis, their vision was largely on forming retail chains for steady market share. Medmen reporting a 95% loss in value is the most telling form of this view. Robert Hoban, in a recent Forbes article, wrote, The Fall of Cannabis Industry Titans is Not Surprising - It's Natural, with a clear point "investors were investing in a chain of liquor stores, rather than the medical advancement of the cannabis industry." The foundation of economic thought of many conventional businesses to enter legal cannabis was indistinguishable from a classical business. The corporate arrogance dismissed the medical stoner operator community as archaic, blinded to the hidden gems of scientific and historical knowledge of cannabis. The corporate business model does not work synergistically with cannabis as a living medicinal plant.

Legacy cultivators understand how important healthy soil is. When you eat a cardboard tasting apple or a delicious juicy apple, the health of the soil is central to shaping those differences. Some Cannabis connoisseurs claim they taste the soil within the flower. We also have scientific evidence that soil with microbial diversity can cool the planet down to balance the earth once again, which is something needed during a period of record-breaking heat temperatures and wildfires.

In a recent scientific study published by microbiologists at the University of Massachusetts Amherst, they showed positive results regarding the diversity of soil microbial to help the soil isolate carbon, which helps regulate the climate and cool the planet down.[6] The study points out the

---

6 Microbiologists clarify the relationship between microbial diversity and soil carbon storage. July 28, 2020 University of Massachusetts Amherst

microbial diversity creates higher levels of efficiency, playing a role in carbon storage. The study continues to prove how important biodiversity in the soil is for planetary health.

The Emerald Cup winners with the best California cannabis flower are always living soil-regenerative farmers. These farmers understand mother nature's protocols. Ecological systems have natural "standard operating procedures" that are efficient and effective and should be the basis of a business model based on commodifying a component of nature. With micro-living soil as a starting point, business models can have a different foundation as well as an alternative framework for efficiency.

If the collapse of the giant cannabis companies is natural, so is the rise of its opposite. The natural rise of a cannabis business model that is synergistic with the structure and spirit of cannabis is in historical demand. I believe it is an unconscious aspiration that many in the cannabis industry have that emerges out of frustration from the contemporary gridlock. If we look for answers to the difficult economics of legal cannabis, we must still start with the plant itself and the soil that allows it to grow.

POLITICS

6. Compassionate Cannabis Programs in California

Cancer patients used to have a strong voice in cannabis. That was before the recreational legalization of cannabis in 2018. The medical cannabis culture of SB 420 that passed in 1996 had cancer patients front and center, at least notably in the Bay Area. The recreational shift of cannabis in 2018 eliminated the grassroots culture of cancer patients and compassionate programs for a heavy retail environment. During the summer of 2019, cannabis activists lobbied the capital and pushed Senate Bill 34, introducing a new compassionate program, which passed through the state senate and implemented on March 1, 2020. According to the Health and Safety Code 11362.7, patients with a valid medical card can receive donated cannabis. The amount of the donated medicine will count towards the total legal amount purchased, pursuant to Bureau of Cannabis Control ("BCC") regulations 5409 and section 11362.77 of the Health and Safety Code. With cannabis being handcuffed by heavy taxes, the BCC explains the compassionate program allows, "cannabis retailers may provide free cannabis or cannabis products to qualified medicinal patients...which also exempts these donated items from excise, sales, and use, and cultivation taxes."[7] Now that this is the law, what do we do about it?

The illicit market is three times bigger than the legal market, which still supplies a significant amount of those with medical needs who have limited resources, and this embodies health risks. Simultaneously, cultivation is trying different market avenues to absorb their product, selling wholesale to other manufacturers for extracts, pre-rolls, white labeling 1/8ths, etc. But excess product makes the growers nervous, and track and trace makes sure

7 California Senate Bill No. 34

that the back door illicit market dump is not an option. Nevertheless, the fierce competition, especially with heavily capitalized companies who have space to play with their margins, pushes the price significantly down. As a result, compassionate based practices could be an economic stressor for cultivation if done erroneously. But for products unsold and still track and trace compliant, the compassion program can be an important valve.

Retailers have an interesting position. The BCC states, "Only licensees authorized for retail activity, or nonprofits working in conjunction with those licensed retailers, may provide donated product directly to qualified medicinal consumers." Many times, cultivators have products that are difficult to sell; "smalls," small flower buds, or high quality trim. If cultivators analyzed their product's quality and volume and created a formula between sales and compassion that protected their operational margins, we can see an interesting opening develop. Setting up such a partnership with retail, where patients can pick up compassionate based medicine, could be groundbreaking. Santa Cruz Veteran Alliance ("SCVA") brick and mortar, which is owned by veterans who heavily support operation EVAC (Educating Veterans About Cannabis), have had a dynamic compassionate program for veterans. Supporting the SCVA retail is supporting its compassionate program. It's in the branding and central to their politics. Dear Cannabis, is a new non-profit dedicated to distributing cannabis to those in need and collecting stories on how it has helped one's health. Farms and retails can utilize SB 34 and help the communities they directly serve or work with, either way developing the compassionate wing of cannabis.

Imagine hundreds of growers and hundreds of retailers forming a parallel system. Retailers could openly educate the compassionate partnership they have with cultivation and develop a medical distribution system for a certain number of patients. Inventory would be limited, so the number of patients would be as well. But any medical patient would feel good knowing their medicine was from a licensed cultivator, tested, and sent to retail directly for medical reasons, especially if buying from unlicensed street sellers is the alternative. Building this bridge would be a politically powerful structure for the California Cannabis industry. It would be simultaneously challenging both the illicit market and the overtaxed retail products. It also allows for the spirit of SB 420 to breathe in the retail world of prop 64, where profit margins dominate.

The inherent medicinal use-value the plant has shaped its agency on the market. The profit-driven forces attempting to capture market share who have yet to contextualize this reality creates an imbalanced dynamic in the industry. Building small-scale compassionate programs that highlight the benevolence of the farmer and the retailer could take place. The political marketing would be powerful for the farmer, who is often marginalized or invisible, and adds medicinal social value to the urban retailer, who is viewed as a cannabis 7-11. Building a plethora of micro-compassionate programs throughout California, structured through an umbrella organization could generate serious political influence, altering how the industry is seen and understood. The medicinal purpose could flourish. The opening is not huge, with high operational costs, but without the burden of taxes. Whether it's the activists who passed SB 420 in 1996 or the activists lobbying work that materialized Senate bill 34 2019-2020, a follow up logistical and political system is needed to give this law the functional heart it needs. Costs for retail cannabis are way too high for working class patients, and the streets always have risks tied to the product. We must utilize everything we can from Senate bill 34, as it's a clear extension of the previous medical movement that birthed proposed 64.

7. Cannabis, Farm Workers, and the Coronavirus

The Coronavirus has made life seem to be reduced to scrounging supermarkets, bunkering down with Netflix, and dealing with more Coronavirus news in this time of quarantine. On March 19, 2020, California Governor Newsom issued Executive Order N-33-20, which only allows businesses to legally operate who are "Essential Critical Infrastructure" for the state. We include Agriculture. Who else will supply the supermarkets we are so dependent on? While we are living our secluded lives, how many canned and dry foods can we stomach without fresh fruits and vegetables?

Roughly a half a million farmworkers toil in California's fields with the toughest conditions. State mandated minimum wage is violated, with piecemeal pay that fosters break violations and speed ups or off the clock work dominates, like doing 9.5 hour shifts for only 8 hours of pay. Farmworker Daniel Castellanos states, "We used to work 10 to 12 hours a day and during the hottest time of day." "This is difficult work. It's for crazy people, as I've heard some youngsters[8] say." Farmworkers doing long 10-hour shifts will collapse in the heat. The pesticides of Monsanto are sprayed with weak protective equipment, creating carcinogenic conditions for the daily work life. In California, approximately 265,000 women farmworkers are sexually assaulted. UC Davis' Western Center for Agricultural Health and Safety claims around half of the farmworker population in California has no health care coverage.[9] The average age of the farmworker is forty-five, getting older. To add to the difficulties of working in these conditions, the Trump administration's suspended visa applications in Mexico, the H2-A agricultural guestworker visa.

---

8 Farmworkers face illness and death in the fields by Ruxandra Guidi Aug. 20, 2018 High Country News
9 UC Davis Western Center for Agricultural Health and Safety, Bleak Outlook for California Farmworker Health Coverage Prospects.

In a period of emotional difficulty with coronavirus deaths on the rise, the Trump Administration is attempting to suspend legal agricultural work during an epidemic where agricultural food is essential for our health.

Even though onion, garlic, and ginger won't kill the Coronavirus, these superfoods are part of the plant based medicinal world that cannabis is a part of. Processed foods versus whole plant foods are radically different when it comes to health benefits. Organic Fruits and vegetables are medicinal in impact, low in fat and cholesterol, and full of vitamins and biodiversity; when you eat a banana, kiwi, or cucumber, you're consuming its life as a plant. Processed meat is deemed as a known and probable carcinogen in 2015 by the World Health Organization. In 1986, Kyriakos Markides wrote a paper that shocked the American academy, arguing that Latino immigrants have a healthier life and life expectancy than their White counterparts, first coined the Hispanic Epidemiological Paradox. A part of the study shows how Latino immigrants eat a sizable amount of fresh fruits and vegetables, more so than their White counterparts.

Since more scientific work is generated on how organic fruits and vegetables fight cancer, increasing organic fruit and vegetable intake will maximize the potential strength of our immune system, which is optimal during our epidemic and picked by farmworkers.

The strongest ally cannabis has is agriculture since it's inherently a part of it. Interestingly, the pesticides they legally use in food-based agriculture are illegal in cannabis. The logic is our liver can filter pesticides, but our lungs cannot, which is problematic. Cancer is the second leading cause of death in the US, and eating conventional food, which is pesticide grown, accumulates in our bodies, and our liver cannot filter out the permanent and constant stream. From this dynamic, the Cannabis industry can positively influence large agriculture in the right direction, making organic production mainstream. The actual practices of this shift would be done by farmworkers.

Exploiting agricultural workers is as American as apple pie. The origins of the H2-A is an agricultural guestworker program from World War II. As thousands of soldiers went to war, women and people of color entered the factories in masses. Black people did the agricultural work for little money, which was not a political option; the government launched the Bracero Program, recruiting 4.6 million Mexican nationals to do the agricultural work for the US economy. The biggest issue with this is the Mexican guest workforce was not paid for their work, and it was one of the largest wage theft scandals in modern American history. American Black Chattel Slavery started the process of depending on hyper cheap slave labor as our agricultural base, starting in 1619 and ending in 1865. Such a system started way before the formation of the US as a country, and it took a whole Civil War to eliminate that system. California cotton was started by some of the same cotton slave owning families in Georgia. The powerful cotton agricultural industry shaped the name of one of its counties: King County as in Cotton is King. Wages for cotton pickers in California had declined significantly from $1.50 per hundred pounds in 1928 to only 40 cents per hundred pounds in 1932. Approximately 18,000 cotton workers struck, mostly Mexican immigrants, that inspired a larger agricultural strike wave in 1933 through California. Approximately, 48,000 agricultural workers for cotton, fruit, and vegetables struck for better wages and working conditions that year, shaking California to its core. One year later, Harry Bridges and longshore workers led a general strike in San Francisco, forming the International Longshore Warehouse Union ILWU, which was a powerful hiring hall and a strong port labor movement. Notably, agricultural workers acted on the necessity of organizing for survival before it was in motion in the cities while working to put food on our tables.

As cannabis is part of agriculture, it connects to our food. Cannabis offers one set of medicinal relief, while agricultural food offers another set. How certain cannabis strains pairs with certain foods for optimal health is a powerful potential to develop. Which strains of cannabis can go with vegetable soup during flu season? Or more specifically with ginger or dates? Pairing is a powerful move, underdeveloped, and opens the door for combinations that are more complex between cannabis, agricultural foods, and the building of new plant medicinal based products. The environment needed for cannabis and agricultural food mix is a healthy and stable agricultural workforce. It took a pandemic to realize if there is a connection. Demonstrating care for the health of agricultural workers will only build a much healthier world filled with healthy organic food and cannabis.

8. $30 Million for California Equity Cannabis Business

On April 21, 2020, The California Office of Business and Economic Development (GO-Biz), with the Bureau of Cannabis Control "BCC", announced it would distribute $30 million in equity cannabis funds. $23 million would go to low interest loans or grants with specific language from the BCC states the funds, "will be directly allocated to applicants and licensees specifically identified by local jurisdictions as being from communities most harmed by cannabis prohibition" (Italics added). The money is generated from the California Cannabis Equity Act, amended by AB 97.

Funds are distributed to cities and counties as:

Local Jurisdiction Funding for Cannabis Equity Applicants/Licensees

City of Oakland	$6,576,705.76
City of Los Angeles	$6,042,014.23
City and County of San Francisco	$4,995,000.00
City of Sacramento	$3,831,955.93
City of Long Beach	$2,700,000.00
County of Humboldt	$2,459,581.02
County of Mendocino	$2,245,704.40
Total	$28,850,961.34

Local Jurisdiction Funding for Cannabis Equity Assessment/Program Development

County of Lake	$150,000.00
County of Monterey	$150,000.00
County of Nevada	$149,999.95
City of Palm Springs	$149,397.90
City of San Jose	$149,300.37
City of Santa Cruz	$147,666.75
City of Clearlake	$98,890.43
City of Coachella	$93,783.26
City of Stockton	$60,000.00
Total	$1,149,038.66

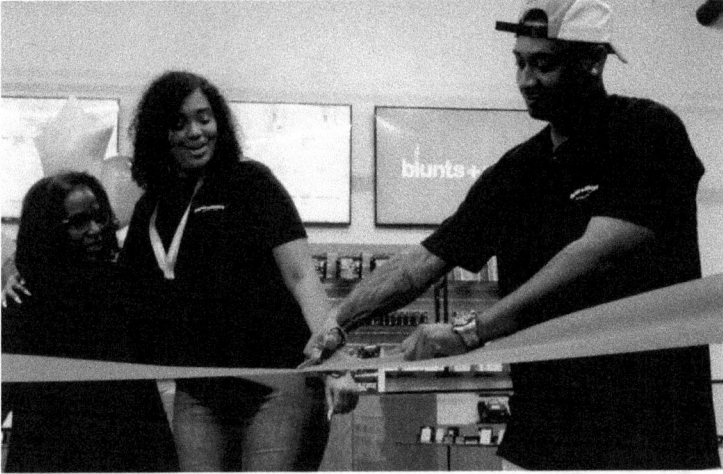

This money is for equity companies to succeed. But will equity success overcome The War On Drugs? The small group of cannabis equity business operating that include but are not limited to, Blunts and Moore, SF Roots, Padre Mu, James Henry, Calibueno, Peakz, Sticky Icky, Maat, New Life CA, Cloud 9, Osanyin, are all struggling to generate economic stability. Having to compete with large, financed companies, illicit markets, and heavy taxes makes the markets incredibly unfavorable. Interestingly enough, Oakland has the most money and equity businesses. Los Angeles and San Francisco's equity programs lagged in issuing licenses compared to Oakland's rapidity. Oakland is in a leadership position in the state, and California is in a leadership position in the nation regarding cannabis equity policies.

It will be important for the city governments to be transparent in its distribution of funds, and measure to what degree they complied to the spirit of the law, which was clear about funds being "directly allocated to applicants and licensees" that are.. "from communities most harmed by cannabis prohibition." When other states form and fund equity cannabis programs, transparency on funds, and social metrics will be key. The established equity companies that adventured through 2018 and 2019 have unfavorable tax conditions in Oakland. Those veteran 2018 equity companies who do come from communities most harmed should receive proportional help. Given that the legal language between loan and grant is ambiguous, we should be open to offering grants to veteran equity businesses as other key companies of other industries receive bailouts. This is not to leave anyone out, but to ensure that people recognize business leaders of the equity movement for their foundational work.

J A M E S

H E N R Y

Even the success of such companies would not overcome the historically deep damages the racial war on drugs had. The US has the largest prison population, with the largest drug possession based violation that disproportionately impacts Black and Latino communities. Most of these equity companies mentioned have less than 20 employees and operate at a local level, demonstrating the success of these companies still would not get close to remedying the damages created by the war on drugs. Nevertheless, the death of these equity businesses would be politically terrible, erasing the dynamic histories of veteran operators who were arrested, jailed, and laid the groundwork for what the industry is today. We must support the veteran equity businesses without illusions of the racist damages in the community. This issue cuts deep in the community, and even though we can't change everything at once, we can begin to lay its foundation.

9. Lebanon Struggles to Legalize Cannabis

The United Nations claims Lebanon is the third biggest hashish producer in the world.[10] But cannabis is illegal under their Narcotic Drugs and Psychoactive Substances Law 673. Lebanon also defaulted on an overdue $1.2 billion bond payment, reaching a public debt that is 170% of the GDP, the third-highest ratio in the world.[11] On April 21, 2020, parliament approved a draft of medical and industrial cannabis use, which made global news as the first Arab country to legally embrace cannabis. Lebanese politicians have been publicly endorsing medicinal cannabis, and in July 2018, Raed Khoury, the Economy Minister, even stated that Lebanon's cannabis was "one of the best in the world."[12] Many Lebanese also call cannabis al-Mabroukeh, the "blessed plant."

---

10 Lebanon Ranked The Third Major Supplier of Cannabis In The World by Nour Abdul Reda
11 Lebanon Plans to Legalize Medicinal Cannabis by Martin Green March 31, 2020 Marijuana Politics.
12 Cannabis Use in Lebanon – Laws, Use, and History

The center of cannabis cultivation resides in the famous Bekaa Valley, which the Lebanese state does not control. During the 1975-1990 Lebanese Civil War, the Bekaa region produced some $500 million a year in opium and cannabis. The Bekaa region is composed of independently armed farmers who praise cannabis, as well as Shia militias and Hezbollah. The terrain developed an autonomous character. The media often demonizes Bekaa cannabis farmers as the 'mafia,' creating a hostile political environment because cannabis farmers defend their fields. When state and police forces arrive with bulldozers and trucks, automatic weapons fire, or even rocket-propelled grenades in response. Furthermore, Bekaa's steady economics draws immigrant labor, a Syrian cannabis worker in Yammouneh reported he made $500 a month, seven times the average salary in Syria. Al-Akhbar, the interior minister of Lebanon, reported, "The government had allocated 35 billion Lebanese pounds annually to aid the farmers, as part of a five-year project for alternative crops to hashish." Farmers have tried apples, tomatoes, and potatoes but would lose money during harvest. Furthermore, 500 acres bring in 9,920 pounds of flower, which they value at 9 million dollars. No other agricultural product can compete with this economic output.

Lebanese legislator Antoine Habchi, who sent the bill to Parliament, said his aim is to "allow farmers to live with dignity."[13] Under the bill, they would tightly control cultivation. Private pharmaceutical companies would provide seeds and seedlings to farmers, and during the harvest, have a strict track and trace system to disallow native and wild cannabis growth. This undercuts the organic strains that have been growing in Bekaa for decades with high amounts of medicinal CBD. Farmers in Bekaa Valley are protesting the move, claiming that the legalization is a "theft from our people."[14] One farmer stated, "As this crop generates a lot of revenues, so our politicians want to legalize it to steal that production." Another Bekaa farmer stated, of legalization, "It will be a slow death." The Bekaa farmers fear that legalization will allow the state and pharmaceutical institutions to take over the Lebanese cannabis. As an owner of a California Oakland equity cannabis company, we compete with well capitalized corporations

13 Bekaa Valley hopes for Cannabis Legalization Jul. 28, 2018 Bassem Mroue
14 Cannabis farmers in Lebanon's Bekaa Valley fight government push for legalisation By Adam Harvey in Lebanon's Bekaa Valley 19 Oct October 2018

and deal with a fear of a corporate takeover eliminating small craft cannabis businesses. The fears are parallel.

If Lebanon is the closest Arab country to cannabis legalization, it is significant due to the historical depths of cannabis in the region. Consider four historical facts of cannabis and hemp in the ancient middle east. One, the ancient city Çatalhöyük, located in central Turkey, is the oldest human city formed around 7,500 BC. Archeologists have recently discovered a baby wrapped in Hemp in the ground, dating back 9,000 years old, making it the oldest hemp product known to humans.[15] Two, the Assyrian empire, existing where modern-day Iraq is, produced thousands of medical clay tablets around 900 B. C. containing prescription for medical cannabis. Cannabis was referenced as Qunubu. Three, Zoroastrian Persia called cannabis Haoma. The Zend-Avesta, one of the most important religious texts for the Sasanian Empire, the ancient Persian empire, has references to Haoma cannabis.[16] Four, the Afghanistan strain landrace Afghani is considered one of the five oldest strains in the world.[17]

---

15 Turkey: 9,000-Year-Old Hemp Fabric Found 02/04/2014 by Steve Elliott Hemp News
16 Cannabis in the Ancient World by Chris Bennet
17 The 5 Oldest Strains of Marijuana by Melissa Sherrard Civilized

Cannabis was deeply woven into the ancient fabric of the Middle East, and reconnections to those developments are key.

Lebanon legalizing cannabis is a powerful step. Developing the economy is important, and how empowered the farmers of Bekaa will be is a key political question. The deep cannabis history of the Middle East shows how cannabis shaped medical knowledge, religion, and industrial practices. That history is key in the contemporary normalization of cannabis in the Middle East and is a useful tool for all those pushing forth its legalization process. Lebanon deserves recognition for pushing forth the legalization of an ancient medical practice. Whether it's California or Lebanon, the internal political complexity never makes the legalization process simple or easy.

10. Police Brutality and Cannabis

The death of George Floyd has gripped the US nation with a militant protest against racist police brutality in cities across the country. Unarmed black people were killed at 5x the rate of unarmed whites in 2015, and in 2019, a study revealed 1 in 1,000 black men and boys can expect to die because of police violence.[18] Cannabis prohibition has been central to the criminalization of Black people and people of color, justifying police searches, and violence. Take Philando Castile, murdered by Minnesota police in 2017 because the police officer smelled "burnt marijuana." [19]

The origins of the American police are tied to enslaved African labor growing and harvesting cotton. Poor whites were given an established authority over enslaved Blacks, fostering a sense of vertical mobility. Controlling Black labor was central, and its method of discipline was murderous to the core of its soul. From 1882-1968, 4,743 lynching occurred in the United States. Of these people, 3,446 were black, accounting for 72.7% of lynched individuals.[20] And this only accounts for those recorded; the real numbers could be higher. In 2015, according to the F.B.I.'s Supplementary Homicide Report, 31.8% of people shot by the police were Black, two and a half times their white counterparts, and 13.2% percent of the population. Again, this only includes recorded incidents.

18 Risk of being killed by police use of force in the United States by age, race–ethnicity, and sex By Frank Edwards, Hedwig Lee, and Michael Esposito August 20, 2019
19 Here's how the police officer who shot Philando Castile described the shooting Jeremy Berke Jun 20, 2017 Business Insider
20 Naacp.org History of Lynchings.

If you adjusted per population, the amount of lynched Blacks during slavery and the amount of killed Blacks by the police are consistent. The racialized state-sponsored violence was continuous and only evolved in form.

Out of the 1.5 million drug arrests in the US in 2016, 80% were for possession only. Cannabis arrests accounted for 43% of all drug arrests for that year, and 89% were for possession alone.[21] Black people are 3.64 times more likely than White people to be arrested for cannabis.[22] Montana was the worst offender, with Black people being 9.6 times more likely to be arrested for cannabis than White people. In 2018, Blacks and Latinos accounted for nearly 90% of arrests for smoking cannabis in New York City.[23] The criminalization of cannabis leads to the criminalization of the Black community; filling prisons and "justifying" police violence.

---

21 https://ucr.fbi.gov/crime-in-the-u.s/2015/crime-in-the-u.s.-2015/offenses-known-to-lawenforcement/expanded-homicide FBI Statistics.
22 Norml.org marijuana fact sheets racial disparity in marijuana arrests.
23 Surest Way to Face Marijuana Charges in New York: Be Black or Hispanic by By Benjamin Mueller, Robert Gebeloff and Sahil Chinoy NYT May 13, 2018

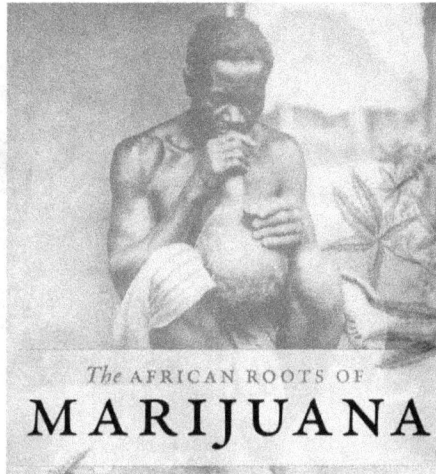

The AFRICAN ROOTS OF
MARIJUANA

The contributions African, descendants have made in the Americas are significant. In the 1600s, enslaved Africans brought agricultural knowledge of Black rice in South Carolina, while in Brazil, enslaved Africans created small cannabis gardens. In many African countries, they referred to cannabis as Diamba and Maconha, terms also used in Brazil, and Diamba has in Jamaica. Colombians refer to Cannabis as Marimba, a term also used in some African countries. Historians are producing more work demonstrating that Africa has a large contribution to developing and expanding cannabis' global position.[24] As enslaved Africans were stripped of all their African connections, so was their connection to African cannabis. Malcolm X was clear with his message to American Blacks that to fully mature, you must politically reconnect to the African motherland, understand, and support their struggles for independence.

---

24 See The African Roots of Marijuana by Chris S. Duvall

The ugly history of cannabis and race is that cannabis has been used to justify racist police violence. The ugly history of cannabis and race is that people have used cannabis to justify racist police violence. The spirit of cannabis is a medicinal plant to be used by all humans regardless of race. Now with the legalization of cannabis moving forward, it must be done by healing and undoing the long history of racist violence and incarceration. Those that are aggressively seeking market share within the cannabis industry also have a responsibility to challenge the present-day injustices that extend from cannabis prohibition. Whether it's George Floyd, Oscar Grant, or Breonna Taylor, building real cannabis equality includes putting an end to the long history of American racial violence. Cannabis will no longer be exploited for racial violence by the police but instead used to generate a world of justice and equality. There is a simple and powerful truth we can learn from cannabis, a plant treats all races equally, our basis for fundamental justice.

11. Ruth Bader Ginsburg, the 14th Amendment, and Cannabis

The cannabis equity community lost a powerful ally with the passing of Justice Ruth Bader Ginsburg of the Supreme Court. Her impressive biographical life has been part civil rights fighter, part legal scholar, challenging gender inequality on every level through the federal legal field. It took the US Supreme Court 184 years to recognize that the constitution discriminates based on gender in 1971, which was one of Justice Ginsburg's cases. It took the law up to 1974 for women to have the right to get a bank account or credit card without a male cosigner; that change was also due to Ginsburg's work. In 1975, Ginsburg challenged the wage system where women who received less social security benefits than men for the same pay contributions, which later became a hallmark case for equal pay. The 14th amendment, historically formed to abolish slavery, was applied to gender, with the equal protection clause, challenging unequal gender pay, advancing gender equality, all helping to form a newer modern human rights framework. With Ginsburg's dying wish being to hold off on the appointment of her seat until the elections, her life legacy is meaningful towards the continuity of developing the legal fight for true human equality.

Her role in society was unique and powerful, always willing to execute a sharp dissenting legal view to the majority if someone violated the principles of equality. She explains:

Dissents speak to a future age. It's not simply to say, 'My colleagues are wrong, and I would do it this way.' But the greatest dissents do become court opinions, and gradually over time, their views become the dominant view. So that's the dissenter's hope: that they are writing not for today, but tomorrow.[25]

Her view of leadership development carries the same principle, "Fight for the things that you care about, but do it in a way that will lead others to join you." We can see a movement forming with Ginsburg's passing.

25 Rabbi memorializes Ginsburg: Her dissents were 'blueprints for the future' By Crsitina Marcos The Hill.

Ginsburg points out the 1776 Declaration of Independence is based off the statement "all men are created equal", while the original 1787 Constitution never mentions equality, which was to suppress slavery as a legal issue.[26] Racial inequality tied to slavery shapes the United States' inequalities, marking the importance of the 14th Amendment, due to the state shall offer equal protection for all those born in the US. Ginsburg's development of the 14th amendment, operating against the state's autonomy, forming the most robust gender equality laws the country has.

Ginsburg legal view of immigration was notable, in the Supreme Court case Arizona v. U.S. (2012), struck down three provisions in Arizona's SB1070, which includes the state's controversial "papers, please" law, a racist swipe towards Latinos. In June 2020, Ginsburg sided with the court's majority in DHS. v. Regents of the University of California, challenging the Trump administration's termination of the DACA program that offers deportation relief to certain young immigrants. Ginsburg helped establish a six month constitutional limit for immigrant detentions, as opposed to Trump and others wanting indefinite terms.

Shortly after Ginsburg's death, on September 15th, The National Organization for the Reform of Marijuana Laws "NORML" filed a Friend-

---

26 A Conversation on the Constitution with Justice Ruth Bader Ginsburg: The Fourteenth Amendment. Annenberg Classroom

Of-The-Court Brief to the Supreme Court, relating to Washington v Barr, which challenges the constitutionality of the cannabis schedule 1 status in federal law. Unfortunately, Ginsburg's passing misses the coming moment of cannabis discussion in the supreme court. Ginsburg's thoughts were always on how much the constitution is a living document, needing modern application from its historic principles. We can only imagine her analytical legal mind analyzing the constitutional violations of the victims of the racialized war on drugs, the scientific facts regarding cannabis' medicinal scope, and the political role of cannabis prohibition, potentially producing some of the most important and electrical legal writings on cannabis.

Her dying wish is to wait until the election for her bench replacement, but her life has offered us a model of struggling for equality through the thick and thin, as a consistent principle laying the groundwork for the minority to make fundamental change. Ginsburg received the nickname the "Notorious RPG," tying her to the late rapper Biggie Smalls, the Notorious BIG, and when asked about it, she said, "Why should I feel uncomfortable? We have a lot in common." Ginsburg's sense of humanity and equality will shape generations to come, a true hero for human rights, embodying values that we all have something to learn from in how we further shape society.

NOTORIOUS RBG

12. Indigenous Dreams and California Fires

The record-breaking wildfires on the West Coast, 3 million acres burned, 33 deaths, shows the seriousness of global warming. California has recently experienced in 2020, six out of the 20th largest wildfires of modern history. Global Warming is no longer a categorical debate among scientists, but the central question relating to humanity's long term survival. Some scientists describe the atmosphere as a giant sponge that extracts water from the land, and as soils become drier, heat waves become more intense,\ and then dry soil fuels fires. This shows how we relate to fires and soil is now so important.

AN INDIAN WOMAN PANNING OUT GOLD.

California state officials recently have teamed up with Native American groups, taking a non-orthodox indigenous turn to fight the fires. For thousands of years, indigenous groups used traditional and ceremonial fires to encourage certain plants to grow, as well as reducing potentially flammable dry substances. To put it in quick perspective, California was born in 1850, and nations lived here for more than 13,000 years. Indigenous societies understood how the plant is adapted to fire; its rootstock remains intact and regrows after a fire. The indigenous fires practiced environmental balance.

When California formed in 1850, it passed An Act for the Government and Protection of Indians on April 22.[27] Three provisions are worth reading from the text; "Justices of the Peace shall have jurisdiction in all cases of complaints by, for or against Indians, in their respective townships in this State." The second, "Any person having or hereafter obtaining a minor Indian, male or female, from the parents or relations of such Indian Minor, and wishing to keep it, such person shall go before a Justice of the Peace in

27 http://faculty.humanities.uci.edu/ Notable Californians Indians Act of Protection 1850

his Township." Third, "If any person or persons shall set the prairie on fire or refuse to use proper exertions to extinguish the fire when the prairies are burning, such persons shall be subject to fine or punishment, as Court may adjudge proper." This demonstrates how California subjugating Native Americans and suppressing all their practices have contributed to out of control wildfires.

These western fire policies continued in 1910, and the US Forest Service adopted putting out all fires. In 1968, the National Park Service lifted its fire ban after noticing a decline in giant sequoia trees, which depend on fire to grow. The Forest Service and the California Department of Forestry and Fire Protection (Cal Fire) slowly introduced fires to control landscapes. California is now practicing fighting "fire with fire," as well as connecting with Native American groups tied to such past practices.

The cannabis industry is deeply affected, and 20% of Oregonian farms have been evacuated or negatively impacted, and endless farms have smoke residue on their cannabis flowers. Rebuilding from this rubble will be challenging. But from a larger viewpoint, there becomes a question of building an economic system that is synergistic with nature, linked to the health of the life of the soil and working with the natural cycles of wildfires.

BAY AREA

13. Towards the Medicalization of Cannabis: Santa Clara County in Tension

As the Coronavirus plagues the news with a rising national body count and historical mismanagement from the Trump Presidential administration, the medical character of cannabis becomes more central to public health. On January 31, 2020 California Santa Clara County recorded the US seventh positive COVID 19 case, and the Santa Clara County Public Health Officer, Sara Cody, acted quickly and forcefully. On April 1st, 2020, such regulations included the elimination of recreational storefront cannabis sales, which affects 16 brick and mortar dispensaries that serve both the one million-plus residential population of San Jose alone, coupled with all their neighbors and visitors it attracts. Oakland based Cannabis attorney, James Anthony, released a petition[28] on April 3rd, arguing that the separation between recreational and medical cannabis that the county made is false, ultimately harming public health, empowering the illicit market, and forcing residents to travel farther to other cities, increasing human traffic. By the evening, the petition hit 6,000 and reached 21,000 by April 10th.

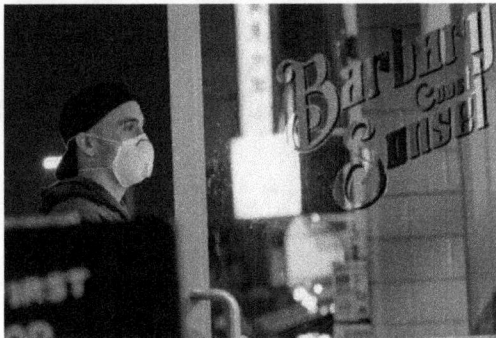

---

28   Change.org Petition URGENT: STOP Santa Clara County from Rolling Back Prop. 64 and Access to Legal Cannabis by James Anthony

Santa Clara County Public Health Officer Sara Cody, trained at Yale Medical School, native to Santa Clara County, and oversaw SARS, H1N1 and other public health emergencies; she demonstrates powerful credentials in medical leadership that should not be marginalized by the cannabis community.

Dr. Cody's leadership has been strict. Dr. John Swartzberg, a clinical professor emeritus of infectious diseases at UC Berkeley, awarded Cody's medical interventions in the county. Santa Clara's Public Health Orders that human traffic must minimize and only essential businesses can be open. The first one listed is retailers that sell non-alcoholic beverages, a frustrating fact for the cannabis industry. The issue for the county is cannabis retail sales can be the distribution of the virus, while the issue for the cannabis community is no different than other essential businesses. These busy brick and mortar dispensaries are a dual sword because they help people receive medicine but can be a center for germ exchange as well. Cannabis clubs should be closely working with medical professionals to set up a system to drastically lower the risk of germ exchange, offering masks and gloves for all employees, mandatory hand washing cycles, and whatever other practices needed. It's a powerful political victory for Cannabis clubs to be considered an essential business, but it creates a serious challenge for the underdeveloped industry. It ties the development of the cannabis industry in the light of the pandemic to developing medical standard practices.

Due to the medical institutions tied to federal regulations, and cannabis flourishing, these two bodies have not worked together. What we can see is the regimented training for a nurse versus the lack of training for a budtender is out of balance. The average training a budtender receives to serve thousands of patients is little, and dispensaries send in sales representatives to provide brand and industry education. As of now, budtenders are in danger with heavy patient traffic if the premise doesn't have medical practices and equipment in place and could follow the lead of Amazon workers and stop the work process for health and safety concerns. If Santa Clara county assigned 16 Health officers to ensure medical based practices were taking place for the 16 dispensaries Santa Clara has, we could begin to close these gaps. A certain specific entrepreneurial drive many cannabis companies have marginalized the medical aspects of cannabis. This virus demonstrates its key for the medicalization of cannabis to take place, both in recreational sales and in medical sales, altering the market culture. Having medical experts look deeper into each dispensary, the ventilation systems, store protocols, medical equipment, the breakroom set up, bathrooms, and cleaning etiquette, it could help the budtenders running these stores during a pandemic while helping thousands of patients get their medicine. Hospitals should be helping cannabis dispensaries. Specifically, for Santa Clara County, having Dr. Cody's medical team help transform the dispensaries into medically prepared terrains could maximize public health, while outlawing recreational sales sends people into abyss, illicit market, or neighboring cities, violating the spirit of the quarantine.

The young legal California cannabis industry formed with medical prop 215 in 1996 and the recreational prop 64 in 2018. It never experienced a challenge like this virus. But the resilience of the cannabis movement has overcome deep criminalization, that enforced creativity with a will to overcome adversity. As the petition states, the separation between recreational and medical sales is a dangerous one and bringing together medical professionals with cannabis professionals is a key step towards solving these problems. It's time for the cannabis industry and medical professionals to move together to unleash the medical character cannabis embodies, all while maximizing and ensuring public health.

15. Santa Clara County Expunges Cannabis Criminal Records while San Jose Methodically Forms Equity

California's Proposition 64 offers legal expungement for those convicted of cannabis, but the legal process is burdensome and inaccessible to most people. San José is California's third most populated city and California's first capital in 1846-1852 and within Santa Clara county. The county also houses Silicon Valley and some of the biggest tech companies in the world, such as Google and Apple. San José also has 367,000 Asian residents (35.7%) and 354,000 Latino residents (32.4%), with strong links to San José's agricultural past. Quietly on the city agenda is the Cannabis Equity policies, a program to overcome the damages created by the war on drugs that have been rising from 13th in priority to 9th. Additionally, Santa Clara County began expunging over 11,000 cannabis criminal cases.

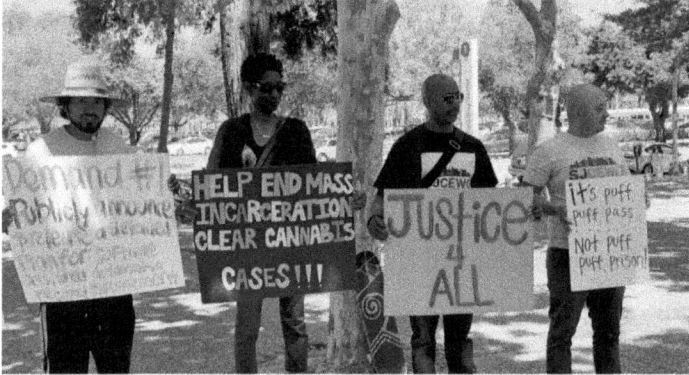

San José State organization Students Against Mass Incarceration (SAMI) organized a protest at the county's building to pressure the District Attorney to drop cannabis convictions in 2019. William Armaline, an associate professor of sociology, and Director of the Human Rights Institute at San José State, shaped the organization. William Armaline pinpointed the injustices the cannabis legalization process has and pressured the City of San José to respond. The San José Equity Working Group, composed of San José cannabis equity activists aspiring to form legal cannabis businesses, supported the cannabis expungement struggle. Jay-Z made news announcing a brand partnership with Caliva, one of San José's prominent cannabis businesses, who also "will focus on and work to increase the economic participation of citizens returning from incarceration." Adding political pressure from a different angle, non-profit Code for America pioneered software to mine court records for cannabis violations and already expunged cannabis criminal records in San Francisco in February 2019. The constellation of forces moved the District Attorney Jeff Rosen to grant mass expungement for the county of Santa Clara.

Supervising Criminal Judge Eric S. Geffon oversaw expungement for over 9,000 people dealing with over 11,000 convictions, making big strides towards decriminalization. "Many families in East San José look down upon cannabis because it is seen as something tied to criminal activity," reported San José Equity Working Group Chair Daniel Montero, who also is a leader of Bay Area Latino Cannabis Alliance (BALCA) and hosts GWSmokebreak. "We have to change the psychology of the drug offender and see how we can incorporate our whole community, in a place where we house some of the richest companies in the world." East San José has not seen the benefits of the wealth generated by Silicon Valley, with the city feeling economic inequality and the police are quicker to push charges to Latinos, Asians, and Blacks for consuming cannabis versus their White counterpart. Eliminating past convictions is important, but if the conditions of criminalization are intact, the actual problem has not been overcome.

Santa Clara's progressive expungement process needs to be followed up by an equity program that would offer licenses and capital to those historically criminalized by the war on drugs. On March 5, 2019, the City Council of San José voted to form a Cannabis Equity Applicant Program and added definitions for equity criteria. On October 9, 2019, the Bureau of Cannabis Control notified the City Manager of San José that they would receive $560,082.30 in funding for their equity program. The city's research found that "interest from equity entrepreneurs in manufacturing, distribution, or testing businesses has been quite low," and that "prospective applicants are most interested in delivery-only and storefront retail due to the lower capital costs and technical needs." The City of San José has had an important focus, where they have seen the "equity face" of a business run by non-equity businesses with the equity owner owning little equity. This exploitation of equity licenses is a real issue. San José is clear; they state, "to ensure that our cannabis equity program has integrity and authenticity. Our program should serve San José residents who were disproportionately impacted by past cannabis prohibition." Considering that it is the same goal the Bureau of Cannabis Control had when it released $30 million in equity funds, and it is the same goal of the equity business movement, an impactful vision can be articulated from this powerful agreement.

If the world felt the power of cannabis culture rising from San Francisco, Berkeley, and Oakland, wait until San José puts all their plans in motion. When the biggest city in northern California can connect its criminalized community with city officials, and perhaps some of the powerful tech firms to help with business development, wrapped around with local integrity and history, we could see some of the most important cannabis business developments yet. But as the expungement did not take place without a concerted effort, neither will a well-crafted and successfully executed equity program that empowers those historically criminalized and matches the high levels of success the county is known for.

16. Berkeley Cannabis Dispensaries Get Shut Down

During this pandemic, cannabis was deemed an essential business, according to the state of California. On March 24th, 2020, the five Berkeley cannabis dispensaries; CBCB, PCC, Hi-Fidelity, BPG, and Farmacy Berkeley, were mandated to only curbside pick-ups. The next day, on Wednesday, March 25th, at 6:21 p.m. City of Berkeley's economic development manager, Jordan Klein, sent out an email to shut down all its curbside exchanges and only allow deliveries. This effectively shut down all the dispensaries. Only one out of the five dispensaries has a delivery service license, Berkeley Patient Group "BPG." City's Public Health officer, Dr. Lisa Hernandez made the decision because she was bitter from a lost political battle. The City of Berkeley's Public Health was against licensing cannabis lounges due to their narrow vision of what a healthy society means for the Berkeley public, and this was a later reaction. The mayor of Berkeley appears to not be behind the decision and one of his aides, Stefan Elgstrand wrote in an email, "The Mayor spoke with the City Manager yesterday evening and had requested that staff reconsider the decision on curbside pickup, and follow the direction of other cities such as San Francisco, which allows this."[29] The City of Berkeley does not seem united on this decision.

Chris Garcia, Manager at Hi-Fidelity dispensary stated, "The City of Berkeley is declaring that these cannabis jobs are not important, unlike Alameda County and several other government agencies who all deem cannabis as an essential business." Blue Reyes, a veteran budtender at Hi-Fidelity, and BALCA member, states, "the customers were happy we were taking things seriously and that we stayed open so they could get their medicine." Blue also mentions the possibility of the dispensaries getting reopened soon.

The idea that shutting down these dispensaries increases public health is wrong. Patients get nervous and go to the illicit market and drive to other cities when losing access to their local store. The City of Berkeley should not be playing politics during the pandemic and should not be scapegoating the cannabis brick and mortar. After a huge outpouring of support and opposition, Berkeley reversed its position and allowed for the dispensaries to operate again. It was clear that in those difficult situations, the cannabis community should unite against problematic city policies.

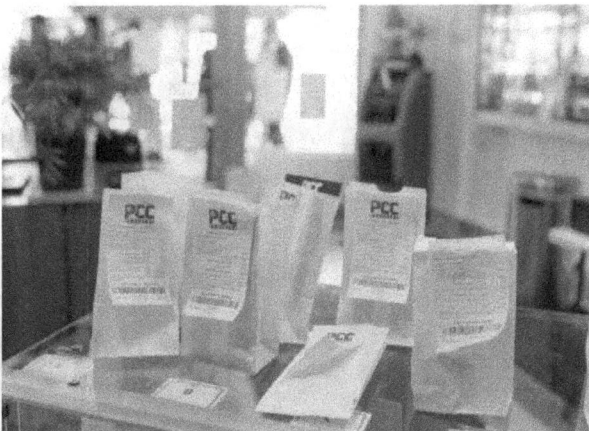

29 Update: Berkeley amends its shutdown order for cannabis businesses; curbside pick-up once again allowed Berkeleyside Frances Dinkelspiel March 26, 2020

17. The New Rising: Ron Leggett's Oakland Equity Cannabis Business

I am the first Native American Equity applicant in Oakland, and I am the first Native American to have a state nonvolatile type 6 manufacturing license.

-Ron Leggett

Native American Oakland equity cannabis applicant Ron Leggett has experienced extreme difficulty and powerful inspiration. When thieves broke into the 45 dispensaries, Oakland dispensary Magnolia Wellness was hit, destroyed, and so was Ron Legget's Oakland equity cannabis business, Chiefing.[30] But what the cannabis community did as a response demands recognition.

Ron states, "It's been amazing, The cannabis community has stepped up and it's been overwhelming, so many people have given inspirational words, I got a lot of help from those who want to help when I was at my lowest point."

JO: What are your next steps?

Ron: I have two products coming out. I have number uno, a preroll, 0.7 gram with a special blend that I hand-picked myself. Shortly after that, I am launching a double-jointed product, two joints in one tube. We aren't going to be sharing joints for a while, so I came up with this idea, it's called the double-jointed. That way, when I buy one, I have one for my buddy.

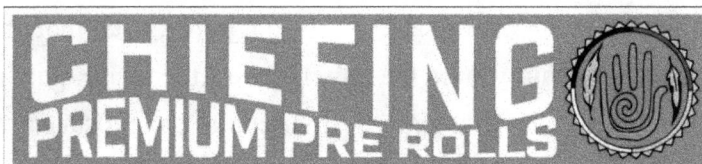

---

30 Weed Dispensaries, Destroyed and Looted in Late-Night Unrest, Face Uncertain Future By MARY JANE GIBSON Rolling StoneJUNE 10, 2020

So many people are supporting me. Someone is donating 5,000 tubes, labels, and a design. I didn't see the light at the end of the tunnel. But many people would say that, and they were right. I am going to move farther ahead than where I was. And I need to give the city some kudos for receiving a city grant as fast as I did. I applied and stayed up to midnight, and the next day I was called by Elevate Oakland for the $15,000 emergency fund for victims of the looting. Debby set up a GoFundMe. I haven't even mentioned the distribution companies who want to help. My long term issue is all the stores who were going to carry my line got hit, the Oakland stores, so I am reaching out to other people who will carry my products.

JO: How have equity cannabis companies reached out to you?

Ron: I haven't had any equity cannabis companies reach out to me. I also haven't had any SF dispensaries reach out either, even though they are supposed to be 20% equity. I am the only Native American Equity applicant in Oakland, and I am the first Native American to have a state nonvolatile type 6 manufacturing license.

JO: As an Oakland equity business, how do you see overcoming this travesty?

Ron: I can only do it with the support of the cannabis community. That is the only way I can make it. I will need help. Some are giving me discounts on distribution. I am asking for a little break to help me get back on my feet, not a free ride. It will help a lot.

JO: How do you envision your business?

Ron: First, it was an Oakland focus; I am Oakland born and raised. Now with the looting, I have also been thinking about other cities as well. I'm thinking of getting another facility somewhere else, somewhere where the taxes are lower, and it is safer. Some of the businesses haven't received the support from the police, like receiving a police report, which is a prerequisite for the city emergency grant.

JO: What message do you have for the public?

Ron: It is an honor to have this opportunity to help others, share my knowledge and skill set to get a license. I want to help others and help them succeed. How do you walk a thousand steps? You start with a few steps.

JO: What issues have you seen in the Oakland equity program?

Ron: When these three-year leases are written; it could take 14 months to get the paperwork together. The city is realizing three years might not be enough. I spent six months getting a permit and planning. They kept giving me all these regulations. Now I have a certified engineer, and the engineer charged twice as much because it was cannabis-related.

CHIEFING
CHIEFING CA | EST 2020

DOUBLE JOINTED

TWO (2) .7G PREMIUM PRE-ROLLS IN RAW NATURAL PAPER
INSTRUCTIONS: IGNITE CANNABIS & INHALE | INGREDIENTS: CANNABIS FLOWER

HYBRID

THC XX% XXX.XX MG | CBD 0.00% 0MG

MANUFACTURED BY: HOLLISTER HOLISTICS 1 - CA STATE LICENSE#: C11-0000986-LIC - WWW.HOLLISTERCANNABI

JO: What message do you have regarding equity cannabis businesses?

Ron: Strengths in numbers. We have been too divided. We had to seek out general applicants to get incubated. We need to build a coalition for equity businesses, where we can share our stories, so they must listen to the players because the players have a voice. We are the ones who do the work. The equity people need unity. When I complain, it's one small voice; when we unite, we have power. We usually go up against high financed companies that we can't fight against. If we do, you need a lawyer, and that costs money. So, if we unite, we can go to the city and the state and push our agenda, reflecting the reality of the situation. The cities that adopted the equity program are getting extra equity funds, and they targeted certain demographics. The system brings in bigger applicants on our backs. For Oakland, they thought it would be one tax code, and then we pushed for a different equity tax rate.

JO: What final thoughts do you have?

Ron: I want to thank everyone who reached out to me, who donated, who sent me emails, so many people out there that there are good people. I want to say thank you to all those people. Thank all the people that have been there. Not once I felt like I was by myself. That counts for a lot of people, including Debby Goldsberry, for taking me under the magnolia wing. I wish the best karma for all the people who reached out to me when I was at my lowest. Anything I can do to help them, please let me know. I'm here for any equity applicants. That is who I am here for; I am here for the equity applicants and want to help anyone who wants that help.

18. Cannabis and the Oakland 2020 Elections

As the nation is gripped by the historical presidential race, a local struggle of complex politics in Oakland exists, and unfortunately, cannabis has been left out. Understandably, the focus has been to challenge the rise of Trump's neo-populist conservatism that has damaged constitutional norms. Excitement exists for cannabis nationally, with Arizona, Montana, New Jersey, and South Dakota legalizing recreational cannabis, and Mississippi and South Dakota legalizing medical marijuana. In Oakland, California, the hottest controversy was Rebecca Kaplan, City Councilmember At- Large, the most powerful politician in Oakland besides the mayor, who was being challenged by Oakland native Derreck B. Johnson. In September, Lyft donated $100,000 to Derreck B. Johnson,[31] part of a larger support for Prop 22 and normalizing gig workers, but Derreck came in second, and Kaplan held her position. North Oakland District One incumbent Dan Kalb won without much opposition. West Oakland, District 3 had a serious race between incumbent Lynette Gibson McElhaney and challenger Carroll Fife, with Fife bringing in a win, receiving strong AFL-CIO, BLM, and housing

---

31 Lyft backing campaign to unseat Oakland Councilmember Rebecca Kaplan Oakland Side September 24, 2020 by Darwin BondGraham

activists support. Incumbent Noel Gallo won Fruitvale District 5, with deep roots in the community. Long time councilmember Larry Reid retired from District 7, deep East Oakland, with five new candidates in motion, with Treva Reid making a win. The noticeable fact is all the candidates, winner or not, did not have cannabis as a political priority in their program.

Oakland is a pioneer in the cannabis industry, whether it was developing medical cannabis under SB 420, allowing for Harborside, Magnolia, and Phytologie to form, or recreational cannabis under prop 64, licensing more cannabis businesses than any other city. Oakland started licensing cannabis businesses before most California cities, instituting the first equity cannabis program in the world, helping those who have suffered damages from the war on drugs. Unfortunately, the older dispensaries agreed with Oakland City Council with having high cannabis taxes, since at the time, there were so few dispensaries. As the industry matured, neighboring cities established lower cannabis taxes than Oakland, such as San Francisco, and the illicit market made headway by avoiding taxes and regulations. It forces us to reanalyze the given tax system. With a new election and new politicians in Oakland, it is also time to renew the issue of cannabis in Oakland.

Oakland's equity program offers incubation with three years of free rent. Some have built a successful business from such advantages. Many have not since the costs of business, a highly regulated system, and heavy tax burden have left them underdeveloped at best. We must encourage the seven city council members to engage the cannabis businesses in their district, lower the cannabis tax rates, and specifically support the equity businesses trying to make it.

Many organizations have formed focused on cannabis policy through governmental policy such as the National Cannabis Industry Association "NCIA," the California Cannabis Industry Association "CCIA," Organization for the Reform of Marijuana Laws "NORMAL," Bay Area Latino Cannabis Alliance, "BALCA," This is Our Dream, LA Equity, Oakland Citizens for Equity & Prosperity "OCEP", etc., but still the layer of cannabis operators involved in political action is limited. Inspiring operators, CEOs, accountants, attorneys, drivers, budtenders, floor managers, to get involved, you can generate coordinated pressure to your city council to lower the city tax, and you can add pressure to your state senator to lower the state tax. With coordination, we can influence state, county, and city policies towards friendly cannabis policies, something needed in California.

If the anxiety of facing a rightwing dictatorship is enough to act, let us not take our local democratic system for granted. We have enough skilled people in the cannabis industry to build dynamic teams to make such changes. Coordinated pressure towards city council, county officials, and state officials is enough to change policy for our industry. But a few loud activists is not enough. We need to show up with numbers and be willing to sway politicians in the right direction with such numbers, unified by a vision. With a handful of dedicated organizers in each city across the state, we would have a powerful network to institute some real change. Entrepreneurs have energy capturing market share; we must also apply such energy to changing policies to allow the market to grow to its real potential.

CALIFORNIA LAW

19. 10 interesting Laws in the Bureau of Cannabis Control "BCC" California Code of Regulations

The Bureau of Cannabis Control California "BCC" Code of Regulations shapes the practice of legal cannabis, but its regulations aren't always the most enjoyable read. The following are ten interesting laws in BCC regulations worth reviewing.

26. Under § 5040. Advertising Placement. advertisement, cannabis companies shall not; "advertise free cannabis goods or giveaways of any type of products, including non- cannabis products. This includes promotions such as: (A) Buy one product, get one product free; (B) Free product with any donation; and (C) Contests, sweepstakes, or raffles."

Promotions that are "buy one get one at a dollar," but it is questionable how long of a life these promotions will have regarding the clear language regarding free products not being allowed. Nevertheless, cannabis attorneys have been applying the usage of paying minimal amounts as legally sound until there is further clarification.

2. Under Code § 5052.1. Acceptance of Shipments. Licensees shall accept or reject, in whole, shipments of cannabis goods. Notwithstanding subsection (a) of this section, partial shipments of cannabis goods shall be rejected in the following circumstances: If a licensee receives a shipment containing cannabis goods that differ from those listed on the sales invoice or receipt, the licensee shall reject the portion of the shipment that is not

accurately reflected on the sales invoice or receipt. If a licensee receives a shipment containing any cannabis goods that were damaged during transportation, the licensee shall reject that portion of the shipment that was damaged. If a licensee receives a shipment containing cannabis goods that is non-compliant with labeling requirements or exceeds its provided expiration date, the licensee shall reject the portion of the shipment that is non-compliant with labeling requirements or expired. (Italics added).

Most retail cannabis businesses reject orders in their entirety with one error. Having a legally compliant way of splitting orders to reject the erroneous portion doesn't make practical sense during busy times, but it is important to know it is legally possible.

3. Under Code § 5303. Packaging, Labeling, and Rolling. A licensed distributor shall not process cannabis but may roll pre-rolls that consist exclusively of any combination of flower, shake, leaf, or kief. Pre-rolls shall be rolled prior to regulatory compliance testing.

That's a powerful card distributor carry and underutilized. The demands for pre-rolls are strong, and a whole new generation of cannabis users don't know how to roll their joints. Pre-rolls is an SKU with a lot of growth and diversity, and in California, there are more distributors than any other license. It shouldn't be hard to find good Pre-roll.

4. § 5307.1 Quality-Assurance Review for Labeling Cannabinoids and Terpenoids. For purposes of this division, any one cannabinoid, Total THC, and/or Total CBD claimed to be present on a label shall not be considered inaccurate if the difference in percentage on the certificate of analysis is plus or minus 10.0%.

So, testing can fluctuate by 10%, and it is still legal? This was one of the big shocks and shows our scientific standards are underdeveloped. We must get testing to be more accurate for this not to be an issue. This creates all types of medical issues for those with strict dosing needs.

5. § 5411 Free Cannabis Goods. A licensed retailer shall not provide free cannabis goods to any person. A licensed retailer shall not allow individuals who are not employed by the licensed retailer to provide free cannabis goods to any person on the licensed premises. Notwithstanding subsection of this section, in order to provide access to medicinal cannabis patients who have difficulty accessing medicinal cannabis goods, a licensee who holds an M-Retailer license, an M-Retailer Non-storefront license, or an M-Microbusiness license that is authorized for retail sales may provide free medicinal cannabis goods if the following criteria are met: Free cannabis goods are provided only to a medicinal cannabis patient or primary caregiver for the patient in possession of an identification card issued under Section 11362.71 of the Health and Safety Code.

The only way to distribute free legal cannabis in California is with a medical cannabis card utilizing SB 34, working with retailers, nonprofits, and microbusiness. This was the spirit of SB 420, before prop 64, generating free cannabis for cancer patients. It's formally illegal in retail for there to be free cannabis, which means developing the SB 34 compassionate act to its potential, with legal limits at hand, attempting to work with the medical community in a collaborative spirit.

6. § 5417. Delivery Vehicle Requirements. A vehicle used for the delivery of cannabis goods shall be outfitted with a dedicated Global Positioning System (GPS) device for identifying the geographic location of the delivery vehicle and recording a history of all locations traveled to by the delivery employee while engaged in delivery. A dedicated GPS device must be

owned by the licensee and used for delivery only. The device shall be either permanently or temporarily affixed to the delivery vehicle and shall always remain active and inside of the delivery vehicle during delivery. At all times, the licensed retailer shall be able to identify the geographic location of all delivery vehicles that are making deliveries for the licensed retailer and document the history of all locations traveled to by a delivery employee while engaged in delivery. A licensed retailer shall provide this information to the Bureau upon request. The history of all locations traveled to by a delivery employee while engaging in delivery shall be maintained by the licensee for a minimum of 90 days.

Delivery services often have small staffs and limited resources. Oakland has a very high number of delivery services. Having this level of documentation is important for businesses to have, but I imagine it is challenging. It stuck out as a serious requirement for delivery services and helping overcome this requirement at a low price is key since many of these businesses have slim operating margins.

7. § 5604. Informational or Educational Cannabis Events. Informational or educational cannabis events where no sales of cannabis goods or consumption of cannabis goods is occurring are not required to be licensed by the Bureau. A person may display cannabis goods for informational or educational purposes consistent with Health and Safety Code sections 11362.1 and 11362.77.

This is one of the most underutilized laws in cannabis. So much education is needed, and brand based education is often too superficial with a product linked bias.

8. Chapter 6 Testing laboratories § 5701. General Laboratory License Requirements. Six official Cannabinoids are tested for with their "CAS number," which means the unique numerical identifier assigned to every chemical substance by Chemical Abstracts Service, a division of the American Chemical Society.

"THC" and "delta-9 THC" means tetrahydrocannabinol, CAS number 1972-08-3.

"THCA" means tetrahydrocannabinolic acid, CAS number 23978-85-0.

"CBD" means cannabidiol, CAS number 13956-29-1.

"CBDA" means cannabidiolic acid, CAS number 1244-58-2.

"CBG" means cannabigerol, CAS number 25654-31-3.

"CBN" means cannabinol, CAS number 521-35-7.

Considering there are over a hundred cannabinoids, only testing for six demonstrates how underdeveloped our cannabis knowledge is. Understanding of all the cannabinoids working synergistically for a real full spectrum impact and what role each cannabinoid plays will catapult our medical knowledge. Noteworthy, each cannabinoid is numerically organized by the American Chemical Society, a clear step towards scientific standardization of cannabis. THC is what gets you high, and THCA is before it is heated, and CBD contains powerful medicinal properties. All three of these terpenes are highly covered in cannabis literature. CBDA, CBG, CBN are not, much less known and taught about. CBDA is the raw material CBD comes from before, thermal decarboxylation, or heating it. Raw green food communities consume CBDA for its anti-inflammatory properties, which could be juiced hemp leaves. CBG, at this point, the most expensive cannabinoid to extract with serious medical benefits shown in treating glaucoma, combatting Huntingdon's disease, inhibiting tumor growth, and killing drug-resistant bacteria. CBN is the sleepy terpene developed in aging cannabis; the cannabis community has been excited about this sleepy terpene that helps you get a good night's rest.[32]

We are still learning the full medical potential of over 100 other cannabinoids with amazing medical potential. Incredible potential medical formulas can be unearthed, and the medical quality of products in retail can take a serious step up, and the application can be more focused. The growth of cannabis medical science will help educate public officials and new consumers to cannabis medical benefits.

9. § 5707. Harvest Batch Sampling. The sampler shall obtain a representative sample from each prepacked or unpacked harvest batch. The representative sample must weigh 0.35% of the total harvest batch weight. A sampler may collect a representative sample greater than 0.35% of the total harvest batch weight of a prepacked or unpacked harvest batch if necessary to perform the required testing or to ensure that the samples obtained are representative. The prepacked or unpacked harvest batch from which a sample is obtained shall weigh no more than 50.0 pounds. Laboratory analyses of a sample collected from a harvest batch weighing more than 50.0 pounds shall be deemed invalid and the harvest batch from which the sample was obtained shall not be released for retail sale. (Italics added)

Testing every 50 pound batch of cannabis adds humongous costs and logistical difficulty for farms to move their product. This is a bottleneck dynamic making affordable, accessible, and scientifically correct testing important for mass industrial efficiency and market growth.

---

32 CBN Is Another Cannabis Compound With Beneficial Properties Sara Brittany Somerset Forbes

10. § 5724. Cannabinoid Testing. For edible cannabis products that are orally-dissolving products labeled "FOR MEDICAL USE ONLY," the milligrams per package for THC does not exceed 500 milligrams per package. For cannabis concentrates and topical cannabis goods not labeled "FOR MEDICAL USE ONLY," the milligrams per package for THC does not exceed 1000 milligrams per package. For cannabis concentrates and topical cannabis goods labeled "FOR MEDICAL USE ONLY," the milligrams per package for THC does not exceed 2000 milligrams per package.

Medical cannabis can legally do large dosing, and companies should think about still serving these niche medical needs. One of the big shocks I remember in January 2018 is cancer patients could no longer buy Korova Black Bar Brownie that had a 1,000 MG of THC.[33] This is a medical niche that cannabis law allows for cannabis companies to address. Most medical patients stopped renewing their cards because of recreational cannabis access, which then disqualified them for medical dosages. Medical benefits for cannabis are strong and underutilized.

20. California Moves towards Licensed Organic Cannabis: The OCal Program

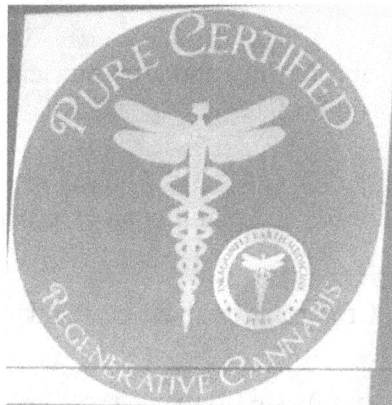

---

33 Last Call: California's High-Potency Edible Makers Crank Out Final Batches Peter Hecht December 27, 2017

The California Department of Food and Agriculture (CDFA) published a proposed regulation to form an organic cannabis certification program. The following summarizes The CALIFORNIA CODE OF REGULATIONS: OCAL PROGRAM. Leaving out packaging, record keeping, track and trace, and other legal maintenance, we will pinpoint the organic agricultural content summarized in ten sections. In terminology, OCal is the term used for this program, not Organic, referencing it as "prohibited from selling, labeling, or referring...products as organic," defined in Article 2 Section 10103. These are the ten sections that define the organic agricultural

character of the OCal certification program:

27. Article 2 Applicability: Section 10105. Allowed and prohibited substances and methods in OCal production.

28. Article 3. General Section 10200. General. OCal Cultivation and Distribution Requirements.

29. Section 10201. OCal cultivation and distribution system plans.

30. Section 10202. Land Requirements.

31. Section 10203. Soil fertility and crop nutrient management practice standard.

32. Section 10204. Seeds and planting stock practice standard.

33. Section 10205. Crop rotation practice standard.

34. Section 10206. Crop pest, weed, and disease management practice.

35. Section 10208. Facility pest management practice standard.

36. Section 10209. Commingling and contact with prohibited substance prevention practice.

1. For Article 2, section 10105 Allowed and prohibited substances and methods in OCal production, references the National List of Allowed synthetic substances and ingredients, 7 C. F. R. section 205.601 and non-synthetic substances and ingredients in section 7 C.F.R. 205.602. The lists are too tedious and long to list.

2. For Article 3. General Section 10200. General. OCal Cultivation and Distribution Requirements; Section 10200, states cultivators need to, "improve the natural resources of the operation, including soil, water, wetlands, woodlands, and wildlife, and respond to site-specific conditions by integrating cultural, biological, and mechanical practices that foster cycling of resources, promote ecological balance, and conserve biodiversity."

3. Section 10201. OCal cultivation and distribution system plans. Focused on eliminating commingling of OCal and non-OCal products. To improve the natural resources of the operation, including soil, water, wetlands, woodlands, and wildlife, promoting ecological balance, and conserving biodiversity. Also, to document OCal seeds usage.

4. Section 10202. Land Requirements states no prohibited substances for three years, distinct boundaries, onsite signage of OCal, and non-OCal.

5. Section 10203. Soil Fertility and Crop Nutrient Management Practice Standard. Growers must improve the soil, not erode it, manage nutrients and fertility through a variety of means; rotation, use animal materials for soil improvement incorporated into the soil 120 days prior to harvest, compost

plant, and animal materials produced through a process that establishes an initial C:N ratio of between 25:1 and 40:1, as well as a list of synthetic substances The National List of Allowed and Prohibited Substances 7 C.F.R. section 205.601, 7 C.F.R. section 205.602. The cultivator shall not use animal materials that contain synthetic substances included in the National List of Allowed and Prohibited Substances 7 C.F.R. section 205.601; nor use sewage sludge for crops or burn crops to dispose of them.

6. Section 10204. Seeds and planting stock practice standard. A cultivator shall use its own OCal grown cannabis seeds or a certified nursery licensed. Except, Non-OCal grown untreated seeds may be used to produce

OCal cannabis when OCal grown seeds are not commercially available or treated seeds can be used with a substance the National List of Allowed and Prohibited Substances.

7. Section 10205. Crop rotation practice standard. A cultivator shall implement a crop rotation to improve soil organic matter, pest and nutrient management, and control erosion.

8. Section 10206. Crop pest, weed, and disease management practice standard. A cultivator shall use management practices to prevent crop pests, weeds, and diseases, by crop rotation and soil and crop nutrient management practices. Also, sanitation measures to remove disease vectors, weed seeds, and habitat for pest organisms enhance crop health, including a selection of plant species and varieties concerning the suitability to site-specific conditions and resistance to prevalent pests, weeds, and diseases. Control diseases through non-synthetic inputs and synthetic substances found in The National List of Allowed and Prohibited Substances C.F.R. section 205.601.

9. Section 10208. Facility pest management practice standard. Pest prevention practices at a Removal of pest habitat, food sources, and breeding areas; using non synthetic substances or synthetic substances consistent with The National List of Allowed and Prohibited Substances 7 C.F.R. section 205.601 through 205.602.

10. Section 10209. Commingling and contact with prohibited substance prevention practice standard. A cultivator or distributor shall implement measures necessary to prevent the commingling of OCal and non-OCal cannabis. This includes packaging materials, storage containers, all containers, or reusable bags. Any materials, bags or containers with synthetic pesticides cannot be used or OCal represented.

The points of action included in cultivation requirements section 10200, cultivation system plans section 10201, soil fertility and crop nutrient management section 10203 become the legal foundation for organic and regenerative agriculture under these laws. Such organic farms produce the highest quality products with the highest medicinal value for the market as well as cool the planet and balance our ecology. It is a win all around, our health and the health of the planet. Consumer support for organic farmers should develop without big name distributor brands who overcharge transportation, marketing, and sales. Cleaner, leaner business systems that tie organic OCal cannabis farms with customers through cutting edge software is possible and needed. Having equity companies educate retailers on organic farming practices will give such practices justice. Big cannabis companies often will leave the farmer and its practices outside of the marketing and brand experience. Ideally, an equity cannabis business can lead the retail distribution and sales if properly educated in such farming practices. This is an element of how we can overcome the damages done by the war on drugs.

The alliance between OCal cannabis farms and equity cannabis businesses could be powerful in transforming the players of the California industry.

21. California Cannabis Appellations and its Importance.

California cannabis growers are closer to establishing on their printed labels the geographical region of their growing, referred to as appellations. Humboldt, Mendocino, and Santa Cruz are known for producing some of the best cannabis in the world with their unique natural terrains. The California Department of Food and Agriculture "CDFA" proposed regulations on February 20, 2020 and incorporated public comment. The Control, Regulate, and Tax Adult of Marijuana Act (AUMA) initiated SB 94, making it mandatory for the CDFA to establish this program on January 1st, 2021. Growers have shown support for appellations, acknowledging it would increase the value of their products.

Under CalCannabis cultivation licensing proposed text of regulations, Article 3, Cultivation License Fees and Requirements § 8212:

Cannabis shall not be advertised or marketed containing any statement, design, device, or representation which tends to create the impression that the cannabis originated from a particular county or appellation of origin unless the label of the advertised product bears that county of origin or appellation of origin. A county of origin, an appellation of origin, or any similar name that is likely to mislead consumers as to the kind or origin of the cannabis shall not be used in the labeling of cannabis unless: (A) One-hundred percent of the cannabis was produced in the named county or appellation of origin; (B) Records demonstrating compliance (C) Within 30 days of the use of an appellation of origin, Notice of Use of the appellation of origin has been filed with the CDFA.

The CDFA is accepted public comment to help form a cannabis system that includes, "standards, practices, and varietals." Specifically, there is a comparison with the wine model called The American Viticultural Areas (AVA), designating wine varietals to a geographical indication. After seeing the established benefits of wine, we can see cannabis has parallel importance. The CDFA lists multiple benefits, such as preventing producers in other areas from profiting from your region's reputation. Ensure producers who use the same appellation produce a consistent product. Encourage the use of best practices in an area. Provide more information to consumers about where their purchases were produced. Help local cannabis farmers stay competitive in the market. Limit additional government regulations, requirements, and fees. Encourage local municipalities to participate in the licensed cannabis marketplace. Encourage existing cultivators to enter the licensed cannabis marketplace. Public comment also weighed in on the strengths of appellations. It ensures the environmental impacts of cannabis cultivation are beneficial to the region and community and captures the legacy of the industry. Provides consumer awareness and education. Creates value for small farms. Maintains innovative farming practices in harmony with ecosystems. Protects craft-cannabis producers through product and market differentiation. Promotes cannabis farming traditions. Supports local tourism, art, and other agricultural sectors.

Humboldt, Mendocino, and Santa Cruz are also known for regenerative farming in their own microclimates. Regenerative farming improves the life of the soil, increasing the biodiversity, which makes for healthy soil, creating high quality nutrient-dense food, or in this case, top-shelf terpene-rich cannabis. Conventional agriculture has had a toll on the health of our farms. We once celebrated The American Corn Belt for its fertility, but industrial farming fostered monoculture systems that exhausted soil fertility, creating depletion and erosion, lowering the farmland value.

Cultivation licenses have been issued across California, but each farm is linked to its neighbors, which could be a conventional strawberry farm that uses heavy pesticide sprays that spread through the soil and air. The best regenerative agricultural practices will hopefully elevate the models of cultivators who currently rely on conventional farming frameworks.

The legalization and normalization of cannabis have undergone a complex difficult process, with the appellations program being one key step towards such ends. The data future cannabis historians can capture from region-specific certification adds valuable information for the maturation of the industry. The legacy growers who have had best practices while being subject to criminalization stand as quiet heroes in today's developments. To generalize California's cannabis best practices to the national agricultural system would be nothing short of revolutionary. Gigantic increases in organic produce, rebuilding super-rich soil systems, replanting native plant species, and rebalancing ecological systems that help cool the planet. From illegal to essential, the more we dig into weed, the more a vision of a better world can unearth.

PSYCHOLOGY

22. Grief and Cannabis

What is the purpose of your life? The question sometimes is easy to answer when life is complete, well put together, and heading towards a clear destination. And in one moment, everything changes, and you find yourself falling down an endless dark hole. Everything that was of importance became meaningless. The purpose of life is unclear, and a depressing environmental energy only offers glim and unclear visions. Losing someone close to you can cause a pain so deep, it's difficult to explain the depths of its impact. Noticeably, the death of one partner from an older couple will often take place shortly after the death of the other partner, and scientists have seen certain animal species do that. It is as if life was composed of loving relations as part of its core purpose. Our society offers programs to advance your skill set in so many directions, but the loss of life isn't one of them. It's almost as if ancient human societies valued the living agency of past loved ones more than today.

The purpose of your life or the perspective you hold can change with the death of a loved one. What you thought was so important, and what captured your daily thinking at a moment's notice, can melt into the air, and your brain struggles to form new ideas of what to value. At this potential crisis moment, many indulge in alcohol and hard drugs as a psychological escape. The emotional horror can be beyond what many are ready to deal with given their tool kit; deep depression, destruction, and despair can overcome us. As a society, we lost important aspects of human connection for the benefits of a fast past market technological driven system. Commodities can arrive at our house in 48 hours, but humans have less skills in dealing with pain, death, disconnection, clouding our understanding of the meaning of our life.

With this said, the role of cannabis for life coping tools is relevant. Many of the sedating indica strains can be useful for periods of extreme pain and mellowing out. Cannabis is an alternative to alcohol and hard drugs for these difficult situations. Introspective, thinking in meta terms, and rearranging the purpose of one's life can all move forward with cannabis. Mental health is one of the underappreciated fields, due to profits not generated in an immediate sense, but it is central to our everyday wellbeing. Most people lack the skills to maintain a healthy mental state of being, searching for cheap substitutes. Clearly, cannabis cannot be a substitute for those with mental health issues, but in a guided way, it can offer support and foundation towards health.

The death of a loved one is one of the hardest parts of life. It is something everyone goes through. When such painful events happen in life, and the world appears to be collapsing. Cannabis administered properly can be powerful to help get through the hardest of times, and offering visions of a positive future, or generating meaning for the present. Either way, the more we explore cannabis, the more we can see the depths of its utility, helping us form a better society.

CONCLUSION

Cannabis touches all aspects of human society, a versatile medicinal plant with an ascending legal position in our world system. Shaping the legal cannabis framework and advancing the education of Budtenders are profound interventions in empowering the foundation of the industry. Budtenders have an incredible power to alter market patterns within cannabis. Budtenders' knowledge of retail could be a powerful political force, shaping policy towards reasonable positions and efficiency within logistics. Budtenders' must feel empowered to take on such actions and being underpaid and undertrained makes such tasks difficult.

As the industry matures, more Budtenders will build an incredible encyclopedic knowledge of cannabis products and their medicinal applications. So many others will be new to cannabis, and unfamiliar with the terrain. I hope to connect many Budtenders who take their role seriously to advance cannabis education for all Budtenders. It would require the encouragement of an intellectual culture, which gets suffocated from the dominating social media platforms. I am confident that Budtenders from around the world could build some of the amazing networks for social change, utilizing the medicinal character of the plant in focused and efficient ways. The 2018 corporate invasion of cannabis, with a rush of Canadian investment, exhausted itself. Many Budtenders are human historians of those wild business processes, unconsciously having a keen and insightful analysis of cannabis retail business.

With a different perspective, one rooted in the cannabis plant, and extensive industry experience, much more efficient systems of operations can take place bringing retail and the farm closer together, valuing regenerative farming practices, contextualizing the war on drugs, creating cost effective logistics, mastering improved business systems, building compassionate programs, are not in conflict with each other as often assumed. The merger of these means the advancement of the industry, solving the serious problems that stand in front of us. Its reflection will generate quality cannabis educational content, further developing Budtenders armed with a higher level of industry practice. I am thrilled to continue this endless journey of writing more Budtender Educations for the future, building this movement from the ground up.

Make the most of the Indian hemp seed,....and so it everywhere

George Washington

"The function of the university is not simply to teach breadwinning, or to furnish teachers for the public schools, or to be a centre of polite society; it is, above all, to be the organ of that fine adjustment between real life and the growing knowledge of life, an adjustment which forms the secret of civilization."

– W. E. B. Dubois

"One can see from space how the human race has changed the Earth. Nearly all of the available land has been cleared of forest and is now used for agriculture or urban development. The polar icecaps are shrinking and the desert areas are increasing. At night, the Earth is no longer dark, but large areas are lit up. All of this is evidence that human exploitation of the planet is reaching a critical limit. But human demands and expectations are ever-increasing. We cannot continue to pollute the atmosphere, poison the ocean and exhaust the land. There isn't any more available."

-Stephen Hawking

"Cannabis is the single most versatile herbal remedy, and the most useful plant on Earth. No other single plant contains as wide a range of medically active herbal constituents."

– Dr. Ethan Russon

www.ingramcontent.com/pod-product-compliance
Lightning Source LLC
Chambersburg PA
CBHW070812280326
41934CB00012B/3161